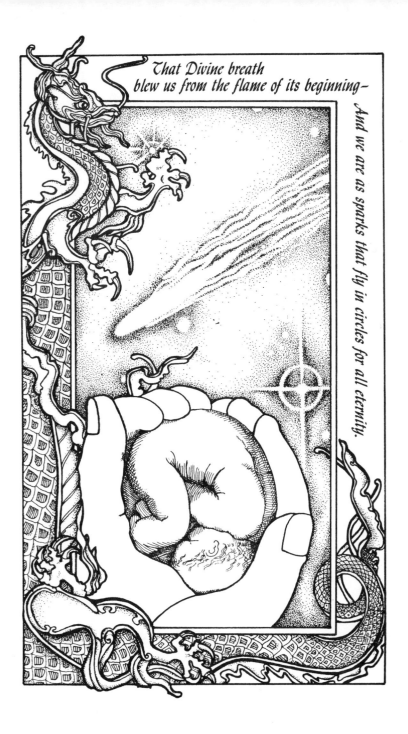

That Divine breath
blew us from the flame of its beginning—

And we are as sparks that fly in circles for all eternity.

Bartholomew

"I COME AS A BROTHER"

A Remembrance of Illusions

HIGH MESA
PRESS

1986

Editing, Design, Layout
Joy Franklin

Illustration
Ashisha

First printing: December 1984
Revised edition: February 1986
Third printing: August 1986

Printed by

High Mesa Press
P.O. Box 2267 Taos, NM 87571

WITH DEEPEST GRATITUDE
TO BARTHOLOMEW

For sharing part of his awareness, with great
Wisdom, Love, and Humor that we may gain in
strength and understanding.

CONTENTS

PART ONE
RELATIONSHIP

PART TWO

SELF

FEAR

That dark and difficult side of human
movement toward Freedom that you choose
to call 'fear' is what I would choose to call a
lack of understanding.

SPIRITUAL BEINGS ON THE EARTH PLANE

'Would you speak to us on what it means to
be a spiritual person?"

TO BE A MASTER

A real 'Man of God' is a Master.

THE TWELVE STRANDS OF POWER

We have often spoken of the fact that you are on
a journey. I ask you now to recognize that you
have the wisdom to take with you the things that
would be necessary for that journey.

ADVANCED ENERGY FIELDS

Emergencies are not restricted to the earth;
as above, so below. With that in mind, I
would like to move into an area that has not
been relevant until now.

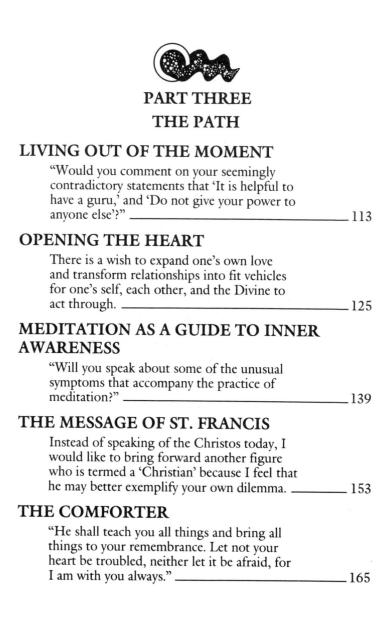

PART THREE
THE PATH

INTRODUCTION

Deciding what to say in this introduction has proven more difficult in many ways than the seven years of channeling that produced the book. The difficulty comes in having to decide which things would be of most interest for the greatest number of people. For example, we could talk about how it all began, how it feels to do the channeling, the things that have been valuable and invaluable about all of this, "Why me?", and on and on. In the end, I made the decision by examining the things that interested me the most and hope that it is so for you.

So, let's start with how it feels for me to be a 'channel' for what is called a 'higher' and 'wiser' level of energy named Bartholomew.

I begin by sitting quietly, calming myself through breathing, feeling the breath inside my body. Next, I set my intention which goes something like, "To the highest power that I am capable of reaching, I pray that You allow only truth to manifest here and may only the highest good result for all concerned. Please help my brother/sister. We are grateful." Then I wait, relaxing into the moment, eyes closed, yet alert. In a few seconds the power begins to build around and in my body. I seem to become more alive, alert and aware. Tingling sensations enter through the top of my head, traveling down through the neck and shoulders and lodging in the chest area. Now I seem to be a part of whatever I am sitting on—no separation between 'me' and 'sofa.' The space around me becomes silently alive. It's as if all the probable questions and answers are somehow contained in energy patterns swirling around me and whoever is with me. When that feeling has grown to a certain intensity, I 'know' we are ready to begin. I open my eyes. Often the room and all in it appear as soft, yellow, dancing light. 'Personalities' are blurred, and fall into the background; 'otherness' moves forward and is easily seen. I have puzzled over what this 'otherness' might be—the soul? the deep Self? the totality of all the loving moments of the person's past? But whatever we might call it, it *feels* like and *looks* like a beautiful, powerfully moving energy expansion which seems to be filled with endless possibilities. It is to that part of us that all exchanges are addressed, and out of which all of the sharing comes.

Then quietly, the energy moves between you and me and forms a sort of invisible roadway that we can move back and forth across. Once that roadway is felt to be established, then the area around you begins to take on various sections. It's as though you are in the center of an amazingly beautiful color wheel, some parts of which are transparent as glass; others darker, less clear. It is to those darker areas that we travel and spend most of our time investigating the contents. It seems to me that one of mankind's main purposes is to increase the vibrations of those darker areas until they are also clear and totally balanced. My awareness moves into that darker area, and 'looks around,' and then words begin to flow. When all of the area has been traversed by us, we move on to the next area.

The chapters of this book have been taken primarily from public meetings which have a bit of a different flavor about them than does a private reading. When there are many people present, the procedure is the same until I open my eyes. At that moment, I scan the group, 'looking for the roadway in.' It appears in a few seconds and I allow my awareness to travel down the open road until I find myself stopped and still and centered. Then—and this is hard to describe—my awareness seems to expand until all of the people in the hall are in that awareness. When that is done, the words begin to come. I state the subject that has been selected the moment before, and then begin moving around 'in' that subject area. It is important for you, the reader, to understand that there are thousands of things that could be said in any of these areas. Because of that, and because I am still learning my craft, I sometimes find myself disoriented by the overwhelming beauty of possibilities. So the first few moments are often choppy and hesitant. But soon I settle down and find my way to where the combined energies of the people in the room most need to have me travel. There is a human element still present here in that I am *not* in a trance nor have I been 'taken over' by some separate entity. My consciousness is very much present but my sense of ego seems to fall into the background and let this bolder, faster moving energy lead the way.

The importance of what I have just said is enormous if you are going to get maximum understanding out of the chapters that follow, because they have been taken from the public sessions and *edited*, not rewritten. This was done in an attempt to capture some of the individuality of what we call the Bartholomew energy. It does not read like a Pulitzer Prize novel, nor was it meant to.

Another pertinent question, is how do we make sense of contradicting answers given to the same question? The answer I am about to give rests on one of the most basic understandings that I have gained from the Bartholomew energy—that there is no such thing as TRUTH in the way that we think of it. It seems that we humans expect to walk down a linear road called 'life' (which often feels like 'death') and assume that when we finally reach the end of that road, we will find in front of us an immense 'Book of Truth,' before which we will sit and absorb its wisdom. And when we have digested all the pages, we can then say that we know TRUTH.

But my work has shown me another view, one that I find more exciting, alive, and possible. And it shows up clearly as I work with another person. When you ask a question, I feel a response that is already a part of your question—so the answer given to one person must differ from the one given to any other person, because any given response is a part of *your* totality, which is unique and beautiful. Another person's totality has different movements of past, present and future and so the answers must be different. In reading the following chapters, please be willing to accept these different views of the same thing. The answers or comments always come out of the energy that is immediately before me, never out of some 'storehouse of wisdom' to be pulled out, ready made, and simply fed into the moment. So, if we can stretch ourselves past our various limited points of view, we all have the opportunity to be much vaster in our sense of knowing and limitlessness.

The final, most often asked question: who, or what, is Bartholomew? My answer has to be, 'I don't know and I really don't care.' I do what I do, in partnership with this energy, because over the years I have found it to be helpful to myself and to others. 'By their fruits you will know them,' and I have come to know and absolutely trust whoever or whatever this energy may be. I believe it to have the utmost love and concern for 'others' while providing practical tools for making our journey "home" more alive and creative.

But there are a few things that I can truthfully say reflect what Bartholomew is:

1) It is a part of me, but greater than me, or who I now believe myself to be.

2) It is energy—this I absolutely know. It is an energy that makes me more alive, expanded, and loving—and definitely more humorous.

3) This energy has a vast range of perception. Past and future are bridged with ease, and grace, and accuracy. It has depth, moving into the vast beginnings of the world and bringing out knowledge that I have absolutely no conscious memory of. The range, to me, seems 'limitless.'

4) The energy has a spiritual flavor, rather than a karmic one. Questions like, "Will I ever have any money?" or "Will I marry Joe?" are best left to others in this field.

This energy's concerns are with giving us tools to awaken from the illusion of our separateness from the One—again and again, this has proved to be its deepest concern. Bartholomew has come as a brother and as part of a universe of equality to remind us all of what we already know—that we see an illusory world of separation, and it causes us pain. But we, as brothers and sisters to this energy, and to the rest of the Createdness, have within us the ability to know the One. And it seems to be Bartholomew's loving job to remind us that we created the illusions and we, Thank God, can end them.

Mary-Margaret Moore—1984

Mary-Margaret Moore spent her first eighteen years growing up in Hawaii and the next five obtaining two degrees from Stanford University in California. She has been a seeker of clear awareness for many years, using techniques ranging from the study of the power of Christian saints to Zen Buddhism. She has been working with the Bartholomew energy for the past eight years and presently lives in Northern New Mexico.

PREFACE

To revise "I Come As A Brother" is not to correct or improve it. The revision came as an opportunity to clarify the existing material and add new, relevant chapters. As this energy we have come to call Bartholomew helps us toward expanding our consciousness, so we feel a greater understanding of his words. This moment is different from the one we experienced when we first edited this book and we hope to use that greater understanding to further bridge the gap between his spoken and our written word.

It has been both difficult and rewarding working with this material. The first objective was to 'change' the transcripts as little as possible, but the deeper we got into them, the more we realized that understanding much of the material had to do with being in the presence of Bartholomew. All our connectedness at those times bridged the gaps in language with ease and we all 'knew' what he was referring to. The same did not hold true for the written word. Going directly to the 'source,' a major concern in editing became to accurately supply the transitions between Bartholomew's explanations, so there would be a flow of cohesive meaning to the work. *All* this without losing the flavor and rhythm of his 'speech'.

The real purpose of this book is to provide the opportunity for as many people as possible to come in contact with Bartholomew's wisdom and love. His teachings are not for everyone, but for those who are drawn to his way, they provide insights into who we are and encouragement to look at our relationship to ourselves, others, and the world, with clarity, honesty, and forgiveness. He comes for a time into our lives to walk beside us in Love, not solve our problems or turn our lives into happy fantasies. He can be insistent because he often reminds us that difficult times give us the maximum opportunity to drop our illusions of separation. He presents his truth in as many different ways as he can in the hope that any one of them will bring the flashes of 'clarity' that we are looking for. He has infinite patience, infinite compassion, and infinite love for us and himself. He points the way and ignites our courage and hope so that we may successfully end the search for our own Freedom.

Joy Franklin – Editor

RELATIONSHIP

There's nothing like a new romance to set the heart singing and the karma flowing.

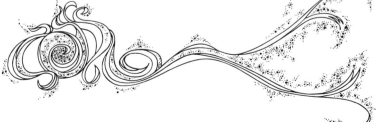

WHAT LOVE IS NOT
3 February 1979
Socorro, New Mexico

I feel that one of your deepest concerns on the earth plane is love, and what love is. It is also relevant to bring forth what love is not since a great deal of illusion surrounds this very simple subject.

Some people feel that there are others that they would say they are in a state of love with. And from their perception, this love is a very strong, deep, abiding means of expression. The word that I think erroneous here is *abiding*. If you will look very carefully at this wonderful, ongoing, eternal 'love', you will realize that it is not everlasting.

So as an example, let us take two people who think they are in a state of deep, abiding love. As they move through their life together, a strange thing happens one day. They have a severe difference of opinion over an issue vital to them both. There are several ways in which they may respond to this situation. For instance, if they are intellectual types, each will argue in defense of their own position. If they are 'nice' people and don't believe in getting angry, they will express their dissatisfaction in underhanded, veiled comments. And if they are emotional, they will yell and scream at one another. These are all forms of resentment and anger, not love. Love is not experienced in these ways and if you are paying attention to your relationships, you will find harsh incidents like this happening many times.

What you consider love is instead a movement of *attraction*. And with attraction comes repulsion. The two exist together. There is very little that can be said to anyone in a state of deep relatedness to

1

another human being who is not honest enough to admit this attraction/repulsion. It is a naive assumption that because you have a great feeling for someone, the feeling is 'love'. When you pay attention, it is clear that many thoughts pass through your mind that are very dark, negative, resentful, and self-centered. This *is* the human condition. So let us go into what love is *not*.

Love is not something that goes on and off like a light bulb. It is not something that one day you have and the next day you do not. That is not love, that is emotion. I would like to remove all of the glamour about love from the mirrors of your mind, because until the glamour and falseness are seen for what they are, and you become aware of your true feeling tones toward the important people in your life, you will not know what love is.

Why should it matter what love really is? Many of you feel that you are experiencing love the best way you can. But I feel that by no means are you experiencing the best that you can. The best is so far better than what you have thus accepted that your interpretation of 'best' pales in comparison. I would like to give you one or two helpful hints that can start you on your own road toward breaking down the illusions about what you do in relationship with each other. A lover who thinks he is a total and complete lover is not going to make any changes. A lover who sees very frankly his area of unloving relatedness is one who is willing to make changes. This takes something very dynamically creative, for once you have seen your own 'unloving' nature, you are opening yourself to the possibility of being taught—which is a very important step in this whole process of becoming Free.

Who will teach you? That depends on who you are and what type of things appeal to you. If you are an individualist and do not want outside experienced help, then use your own mechanism to teach yourself. It is a hard, difficult path because you are not able at all times to distinguish between the real and the unreal and you can easily get into tributaries that will bring you into very dull, marshy, uncreative areas of life. The most obvious thing is to find a temporary 'authority' who has blazed a trail before you, and relate to it as best you can *in your own way*. This leaves many paths open. The authority can be a living 'Master' or 'Guru,' but they are not the only ones available to you. Many 'wise ones,' now dead, have left very obvious trails behind them, and all you need to do is to contact them through books. Go through the list and find one who harmonizes with your own being, and use him or her to help you in your push toward Love.

So, you need to discover those areas within you that express themselves in unloving ways, and then find an 'authority' who embodies the reality of the Love that you are looking for. It does not have to be someone who is still on the earth plane. Please understand that the illusion of separate bodies is yours, and that it is not the highest perception available. Because someone is no longer in body form does not mean that their dynamic, creative wisdom is not available to you. Where would this wisdom go? It is always available in the great sea of Consciousness, permeating and extending past and beyond it. Great truth and wisdom never die. They have a momentum and velocity within themselves that move throughout the Createdness. So be aware that if you feel an attraction toward a path or a truth, that truth is still, in your words, 'written' in the 'etheric,' the ethers. It can still be drawn upon and brought back into dynamic awareness. If, for instance, you decide that the way for you is the way of the Christ (or 'Christos'), understand that His Wisdom and Love are still available to you. I am speaking of the dynamic, creative wisdom that is embodied in His Truth as it was given in the early times, not the reinterpretations that pass for His truth now. And anywhere along what you call 'the continuum of time' that any of the followers of the Christos have been able to dynamically tap into this truth, they have been able to keep this momentum going. This is what a great student does for a great teacher. He takes in, understands, and embodies that teaching, and then by his own attention and experience of it, he keeps it alive in an on-going state. In your

3

words, he 'passes it on.' So the student is doing a great service by being the embodiment and fulfillment of that teaching. In moving it out onto the earth plane, a more dynamic understanding of that original teaching is possible. Thus, any of those great ones who have dealt with these bands of dynamic Wisdom are today still available to you.

When you pick your Path and become centered on that Path, if you will be humble enough to open up your being and *ask* that the Wisdom come to you in some form, things will begin to happen. And they will happen in various ways. You will find books that were given to you years ago now have an attraction. Or one that you have already read will come to your attention, and you will take it up and learn from it in new ways. Friends will give you things, and you will hear new ideas. All of this may appear to happen on the earth plane in very mundane ways, but you should give due attention to them. If your thrust toward Freedom is sincere, you will find that the Vastness will try to expedite your way toward it. People will 'come out of the woodwork' who you never dreamed were there. All kinds of events will take place, but you must be aware that the way they happen is not by some caprice. What really happens is that you have put out a call, strongly, within your being that says, "Please help me. This is what I need." Once you align yourself through your yearning, it starts to happen.

Now, what does all this have to do with Love? It has everything to do with Love, because Love is not something you do, or something that you contrive. Love is something that you allow to have its movement through you and about you. Your very *being* is Divine Love. This is not something that you are aware of, for you have attached your vision to such a limited meaning of what Love is that you are caught in unreality. You think that love is one body caring for another body, or caring for a few other select bodies around you. This is nonsense. Love is not something that you do. In a state of Love, the one fact that you are constantly and utterly aware of is that *Love is something that you are*! And you cannot 'are' something.

Love is your very essence, it is your very Being, and you have no control over it, for *it is* what you are. It is given, in the sense that is has been given to you by the Source. And out of it all things are created. So when you feel yourself to be in a state of Love, you will also realize that it is something totally out of your control. No matter who comes into your vision, Love is a reality in that moment. The strangest people can come into view and you will feel that upwelling of compassion and understanding that is Love. And this may come as a surprise, because you are so used to making very selective choices about the people that you will or will not love. There are many moments every day when upwellings of compassion and caring move through you. These are not always large movements directed at other people, but can be small flashes created by 'ordinary' things. They are embedded in the fabric of daily events, whether or not you are aware of them. If you turn your attention to these feelings and away from your day to day altercations, they will seem to grow and fill more of your life.

In speaking of Love, remember that *you* cannot do it, *you* cannot will it, and *you* cannot demand it. All you can do is to begin to follow a path that you hope embodies it. And as you move deeply into the understanding of what you are and of what you are not, you will become aware of this reality of your life. And when the illusory veils begin to fall, the dynamic power that enters is the Power that you call Love. This power is one of the major movements of the Divine Source, and as it moves through you and out into the world, it gains in its velocity, and is something you can observe. You will see Love in action. There is very little Love in action on the earth plane, because most of the love going on is very personal. If you feel you are a loving person, please look at that view of yourself very carefully. One of the greatest illusions that the ego most enjoys putting before you is the thought that you are a 'loving human being.' Love used in terms of sexual attraction, friendship, or parental instinct can be a device of the ego to make you feel that every day you are becoming more loving. How do you know if you are a loving person? It is so simple that it will be painful. You are a loving person if everyone who comes before your mind, or passes before your view, is one with whom you can feel compassion and understanding.

Most people feel that they are successful in the world if they are able to make money and be in a state of 'love' with other people. These things are part and parcel of the earth plane illusion. At this stage, many of you feel this emotional 'love', and you take it for Love. If you are willing to sublimate your life to another person, look closely at this. If that person were constantly to say unkind things to you do you think that you would still feel beautiful, harmonious love with them? What usually is happening with this type of love is a matter of what you are getting out of it. As long as you get something, even if what you are getting is not positive, you will continue on in it. But if the situation changes to such an extent that it no longer conforms with what you truly want, then you say you are 'falling out of love'. Any relationship, my friends, that you can fall into, you can also fall out of. Anything that comes and goes, as do these ego-based feelings of love, is not the real thing. The test as to whether something is representative of the Source, or is simply another illusion of the ego, can be made by holding any of your feelings or your thoughts for a moment and asking, "Is this feeling *always* with me, no matter what else is present?" If it is not, understand that it is simply another piece of the rising, falling play of createdness on the earth plane, and has nothing to do with the real Createdness of the Divine. As such, it does not really need your attention. You can use this as your criteria for all that happens. If you hold an event in your mind for one moment, you will be able to know whether the thoughts and feeling tones surrounding it are always there. If it is so, then the feeling is truly part of the Whole and should be given due reverence in your mind.

Again, I say that you cannot make yourself Love; you cannot will yourself to Love, because you already are Love. But what you *can* do to get in touch with this state, is will yourself to *want to love*. This is within the ability of every human being. You can change your view of yourself, your relations with other people, and your relationship to your world, by willing yourself to want the 'everything' that you are! If you do not believe this, please give due consideration to the state of love you are now in. Ongoing Love does not come and go, *it is* and that is the hallmark of its reality. Find your own way. Then will yourself to want to Love for that is the key that can show you the path. At the end of any legitimate Path you will find both a state of Wisdom and a state of Love. These are two sisters that go with all states of true seeking. No matter how austere the path at the beginning, at the end comes the Love. No matter how heart-oriented the path at the beginning, at the end must come the Wisdom. They are two sides of one coin and they cannot be separated in any way. Whatever path one chooses to follow, at the end of the journey, it is both Love and Wisdom that will manifest. It is your responsibility to be selective about the path you choose. Do not allow yourself to be taken in by any guru or teacher who does not embody in himself or herself both states of Love and Wisdom.

There isn't any formula for the creation of Love. I can only repeat: *you already have Love moving through you.* If you do not pay attention to it, it doesn't matter if Love is there or not. Unless it is helpful in your life, that Love might as well not exist. It is the state of deep, constant Love and abiding caringness for all things that you seek. You must understand that the responsibility lies with you, to discover that you are not now in that state. Please give all due heart and mind to the need for finding that state of Love within your own being. It is a part of the Source and therefore it is part of you. The illusion that you are a separate body, with a separate mind, somehow separated from the Source of what you are, is not the truth. Take seriously the thought that you are Love. You are Love and if you *are* that, it stands to reason that you can *know* it!

SOUL-GROUPS
22 June 1983
Albuquerque, New Mexico

I have been asked whether, in the incarnative pattern of man, there is a tendency for you to come onto the earth plane in 'clusters' or groups, just as individual cells cluster to make up different organs and structures of the body.

It is clear on the earth plane, that you feel attracted to some individuals and not to others. Some of you also feel that part of your purpose here is to somehow find your 'soul-mate': the one other person who would make you complete. This has rather dismal prospects. Not only must you spend your life searching through billions of people to find that particular one, but you have set yourself up for unhappiness if after finding that one person, he or she leaves you, or dies.

Without question, you enter this incarnative cycle with what we might call a 'group soul.' Of course, there really is no such thing as a 'group soul,' but we will pretend that it is so, to make a point. All this means is that there are 1,000 or 10,000 (you can play with numbers if you wish) souls who come as a single vortex of energy; and when this energy enters the earth plane, they manifest as individuals and begin their process. It is a fact that some of you are faster learners than others—and that some of you enjoy the game of illusion so much that you will continue it, even while others of your 'group' wish to end it. Some of you have even sat at the feet of the Buddha and are still here! And why? Because it has been fun, has it not? Others of you have selected roads so hard and rocky that you have come to the place where you want out, and you want out of the illusion *now*.

As you move through your lifetimes of incarnative patterns, part of the time you choose to be very close to those in your 'soul-group,' and part of the time you choose to walk alone. If you are challenging yourself to a difficult life, you may not find yourself surrounded by others who love and support you. Some of you are very nice people and wonder why you do not have great love in your life. When you decide to go for a challenging life, you also decide to isolate yourself from those energy fields that give you a feeling of support. For in the end, the only place that you can go for your support is to the 'God within.' You have learned as you have moved through many lifetimes with others who love you, that the net result is happiness—so much happiness that you sometimes fall asleep! Fine; everyone needs a rest, everyone needs to go to the Bahamas or Hawaii for a lifetime. But there are also the steppes of Russia for you to live through.

On the unseen planes, constantly present, there is an amazing amount of supportive power for each and every one of you. Part of the job of a soul entity, when not in body form is, to give some of its awareness to those who have incarnated, to give them love and support and sometimes a good 'kick in the pants' when it is needed! Some of your very best promptings, hunches, or insights have come from your 'discarnate' friends. And why is this important? Because one of the saddest aspects of being a human is your belief that you are alone, and that God is so far away as to be unreachable. But you do not say that about your friends. So the point of understanding the 'soul-group' is that it gives you another reality to turn to when you are in extremity. The help for which you look is not far away. Do not place it in the hands of some remote God, for then you will spend many years searching for that God in quiet desperation. You make such a division between friend and God; friend is friend, but God is awesome. He is far away, hard to reach, and very particular. The fact is, that it is you who are very particular, not God. God couldn't care less about what you do, or think, or say, because He knows exactly what you *are* and He knows that you will always be what you are, no matter how many roles you may choose to play in the earth drama. He knows *who* you are when you are on stage and off.

Some of you have been perplexed by your friendships. You wonder why there are people who seem so different from you filling your life, while those who are more like you do nothing. You wonder why it is that any number of difficulties can come up between some people and everything works out; while between other equally mature people, nothing works out. Communication with others of your soul-group is easy—though it may not always be fun. When you have relationships that are honest and straightforward, whether friends, mates, or children, know that you are in touch with a part of your soul-group. They are that part of you that knows you so well that they have the ability to communicate easily with you. Soul relationships can be hard, for they continue to show you a side of yourself that is not always sweet and loving. And those are the sides of your nature that your soul-group knows you must come to accept, for when you do, you can all move quickly to the Freedom that you seek. It is as though you have made a pact with each other: "When I go to sleep, wake me!" "Fine—and when I go to sleep, you wake me!" And when you awaken, you will find as a human that you contain it all.

We have spoken before about the fact that life has both 'positive' and 'negative' aspects and always will. Your job is not to stay at either end of those polarities. The basic substance of the universe is energy, and energy is always moving, so when you try to stay at one pole, lack of movement is the thing that gives you the most pain. When you leave the positive pole and start to swing toward the negative aspect, things become difficult and you at once ask yourself, "What did I do wrong?" Would you say that to a ball which you throw up into the air? Would you tell the ball that it was all right as long as it was moving upward; but was wrong when it began to move down? You do not ask that, for you know that the ball will go up and it will come down. In fact, if it did not come down, you would then ask what had gone wrong! But when it comes to your own life, you refuse to allow yourself that same natural swing from up to down, from one pole to the other. Part of the reason for this is unfinished business from when you were young. The parent says, "What's wrong with you!" The child responds, "I don't know, I feel sad, lonely, and scared." And the parent says, "Well, go do something, and you'll feel better!" Or, "Go watch TV, and you'll feel better!" Or, "Have a piece of cake, and you'll feel better!" Never are you told that it's all right to feel sad, lonely, or scared; that you *can* understand it, and become one with it, and that you are big enough to hold all of your feelings. You are big enough to contain both poles of that polarity because *you are both of them, and something else besides*. Your misery comes when you tighten up, when you do not allow your agony to move. You do this a lot of the time. It is the one place where you could most help each other and don't. When someone is in a bad mood, most of the time you want them to change it, for it is very inconvenient for you. This is telling the person that the only way they are acceptable in this world is when they are happy, positive, and compassionate. The more that you believe that you should be isolated when you are in a bad mood, the worse you feel. Your mind tells you that the only way to be acceptable is to be smiling and cheerful—and so even when you are miserable, you try to look as though you are smiling and cheerful. And you learn at a very young age how to present this face.

The way out of this 'dilemma,' is to be courageous enough to experience directly, within yourself, your negative polarity. Your job is to *know* what is really going on within you. If those of you who think you are spiritual really believe that you have the capacity to be only 'positive,' I would ask you to look at the nature of the world into which you have incarnated. It is a planet of polarity. All worlds are not so polarized. It is the basic essence of this planet. You will not be able to move in it freely until you recognize that. It is part of who you are—and it is wonderful. It is wonderful to move from happiness to depression, *when you are moving*! It is when you are *not moving* that you become afraid and take that fear into your body, which becomes rigid, stiff, and constricted. What is arthritis? Fear of movement. So be very careful because your body will help you not to move when you tell it *that* is what is needed. Whatever you feel, the body will out-picture for you. Be honest with yourself, about yourself. Look honestly at *both* sides of your nature. Allow yourself to realize that you are a 'polarized entity'—that you contain both positive and negative poles. You must be willing to accept the polarity in all things. Whatever is going on in your environment you are capable of handling and if you do not believe it, it is because you have not looked at yourself. You are trying to remain at the positive pole and be 'holy.' You may try, but the pendulum will have to swing back again.

Enlightened ones are very rarely holy. In fact, they are often so outrageous that people look on them as crazy. And what is this quality that makes them appear crazy? They do what they *are moved* to do, and leave you to deal with your reaction to it! They have the capacity to just *be human* . You can tell how close to Enlightenment you are by asking the question: How many people in my life do I allow to be anyway they might wish, under any circumstance, no matter what the appearances may be? Enlightenment is nothing more than the realization that there is only One—that concepts of good and bad have no meaning. When you refuse any of the energy fields that surround you, feeling that you are too good or too spiritual for them, you have cut yourself off from a part of the One. Can you accept and acknowledge that it is *all* part of you? Can you get out of your 'holiness' long enough to *feel* anger, rage, jealousy, or whatever other 'negative' emotion arises? The sign of a mature entity is one who acknowledges the pull of all energy fields and makes the decision whether to follow a particular energy or not. They see *choices*. If you say that you are not capable of some kind of negative response such as anger, then I would say that you have not lived. You do not understand the great drag on your energy that such a false view of life produces. When you decide that you have to be a certain way or no way and cannot allow yourself to be any other way, life stops. Though you may be moving in time and

13

space, your energy has stopped and you can no longer feel that movement. You do not feel much at all. The release comes when you allow the pendulum to swing, and when you move between the poles with ease, you will understand that *the beauty of life is its motion*. The beauty and the power and the joy of life is not in *what* happens, it is in the motion, in the movement, in the constant changing of *all* that happens. Joy is in the incredible dance of Life!

If you are a friend to others, I would ask you to begin (or continue) to allow those around you to really be who they are. And if you are a friend to yourself, please allow *yourself* to be who you are. Everyone can know who they are and you will never find peace of heart until you allow yourself to be who you are. All the rest is 'show business.' It is never too late to be yourself. And it begins with being honest with yourself about yourself, and your unfinished business. Whenever fear arises within you, there is unfinished business there also. Find out what you are afraid of, for whenever there is fear you act falsely. You become afraid when you feel that you lack something that you need, or that you will lose something that you have. You do not need to be afraid of losing *anything*, because you *have everything*!

Let us talk about this concept in the perspective of soul groupings. At the beginning of the group life experience, a part of the group power is the ability to communicate by mind. Even if part of your soul-group is no longer present in body form, you have not lost them due to this shared ability. When one of your soul-group dies, if you have been close, they will not seem to be gone because the communication between you is still open and clear. There is a loss, but the *knowing* is there that the entity is still present. Each entity in a group has taken a different part in the earth experience, so between you, you have done it all. So, for instance, if you move into illness with fear, there are those around you who have had the same experience and have been victorious over that fear. The only thing that you need to do, is to be still enough to listen. You will hear guidance of a nature that you cannot now imagine. Some of this 'guidance' you have attributed to God. This is true in the sense that everything is God, but there are different kinds of messages. The Divine Essence is not going to tell you step by step how to work through your life problems, but that nucleus of soul-essence will. Do you want to know what your next step should be? Would you like to have some hints about what might be down the road? The group soul wants compassion and communion between you; and why? Because *they* can't move on until *you all* move on. In your group, each of you went your own way and then after many lifetimes shared the desire to go beyond earth experience. It is not that *all* sentient beings have to be saved before any *one* can go; but without question, all those in an individual group vortex of power move on together. So in a very personal sense, your soul-group is concerned with your awakening. They are more concerned than the Divine is, to get you 'Home,' because they are wanting to go, while the Divine is already there. This is the most positive thing that I can tell you, for on the earth plane and beyond, you will always have a vortex of power available to help you.

People have asked who I am in relationship to Mary-Margaret. It is possible that I am the Enlightened part of her soul-group, and it is possible that some of you are in that same group, and it is also possible that I am here to ask you to hurry, so that we can all move on.

If you will dwell upon the acceptance of polarity and the possibility of 'soul-groups,' you can present yourself with the opportunity to drop self-pity, feelings of loneliness, and the fear of not knowing how to live your life, because you have access to a group of experts. The energies around you constantly tell you what they know, so all you have to do is listen. Listen to the messages while you are awake, and listen to them when you are asleep. Soul-group energy comes to help you in your dreams. They alert you to what you most need. These are the 'power dreams' that speak to you with clarity and in a way that you can understand. Do not have the idea that this 'other world' is 'over there,' and you are here; so until you die, never the twain shall meet. It is often easier to communicate and share with your soul-group energy than with another embodied person, because your group is closer to you. It constantly surrounds you. It may touch you as a brief vision, or the awareness of a 'guardian angel.' There is within your group an 'enlightened one,' or perhaps more than one, with whom you can share. When you feel that you can communicate only with other entities in physical bodies, you have cut yourself off from a powerful source of inner guidance. So, take it or leave it. We will wait! But there is a tremendous desire to move beyond one's boundaries, to expand farther and farther, and in the end, this is why parts of your group come to you.

Your own group energy field or vortex has the capacity to see vastly, and so it can feed you information which is beyond your sensory, egotistic, and mental apparatus. You are so much more than your believe you are! You think that you are only one small person with a capacity to join with one other or a few others. And that is a lonely view. I am trying to break down that limitation and encourage you toward a much vaster view. Once you understand and experience yourself as part of a Wholeness of energy, of Oneness, then you are ready to move with that knowledge. But stuck in the belief that you are one small person, alone, unconnected, only cared for if others decide to, you create a feeling of isolation and dependency. Once you begin to believe that there is help 'out there,' you will know it to be true. But until you do, no matter what comes through, you will doubt it. As long as you believe that you are a person who needs to have pain and suffering, you will have it. When you decide that you are a person for whom joy and happiness would be maximum, you will make another choice. Practice awareness! When you awaken in the morning, before the drama of the day moves into your consciousness, stop and ask for that knowledge you seek, and you will know.

There is, within the soul-group, an intimate caring. Intimacy has little to do with bodies, it has everything to do with souls. And your 'soul' can be deeply intimate with hundreds of energy sources.

16

There is no reason for you ever to feel helpless or alone. You are so locked into the belief that you cannot allow intimacy except on the physical level, that you have trapped yourselves. Physical intimacy is wonderful, but I will tell you, it is not all that you are seeking. It can be found in the body, but the physical does not create it. Please understand that at every moment you have the power to reach out and bring to you the comfort, the wisdom, and the humor that you seek. This energy gives you space to *be*, to *love*, to *enjoy* yourself! You are worth *everything*. The sooner you know that, the sooner you will begin to manifest it.

Q: How can we accept the negative side of our polarity?

First we must explore what negativity means to you. Let us set up a scenario: you have just had a terrible fight with someone that you care deeply about. They have said things that hurt you, and as the words enter your being, you begin to draw a mental picture from out of your pain. Your emotions draw a picture of anger and resentment. You then respond to the picture, believing it to be real. But what you have not done is ever doubt the validity of the picture. You feel the pain and you feel like screaming and crying. Stop at that point, and sit in those emotions, feel them and *allow them*. Out of that allowing, different movements will begin to happen. You will pass through the emotional level of the picture into the real energy that stands behind it, and you will begin to release those emotions.

You stop at the picture level because you are afraid to release the emotions you are feeling for fear that they are not acceptable. So you don't act, and that energy stays stored within you. What is necessary is to stay in the moment to moment, allowing and feeling the different energies move you past the 'picture' to the essence of the drama. When you by-pass the picture, you will learn something. Energy is there, but suddenly it does not feel so bad. And it does not feel so bad because *all* energy is the Divine in motion. What is *not* Divine is your picture of anger and resentment—your

17

negativity. When you by-pass the picture and move directly to the energy, it feels the same as joy and beauty and harmony. It feels the same because there is *only One energy*! As white light passes through a prism as one color and moves out as many, so it is with you. The energy comes in as one, and since you are the 'prism' through which it moves, it spreads out into different bands—into action, thought, emotion. If you will remain steady as the prism, and feel the energy *as it comes in*, you will feel all right! You will know the energy of the One and not the fragments of the picture.

My dear friends, I have been screaming at you for so long, and I love you so much. The conditioning in all of you is so heavy; you are conditioned *not to feel*, you are conditioned to react. Conditioned response means that you are trapped within your 'picture.' And it is a horror movie! Go to the feelings, and in the acceptance of the feelings, the release begins. Do you understand? Man spends his whole life running from feeling with the mistaken belief that you cannot bear the pain. But you have *already* borne the pain; what you have not yet done is to feel all that you are beyond that pain. *That* feeling has a movement to it. When you stop the reality of that motion and go to the fantasy of your fear about the 'swing,' you have placed yourself in a trap with no movement possible. The feeling is the part of you that is *in motion*, and it cannot stop. The emotion comes and goes. What you need is the willingness to sit with yourself and discover this.

Many of you think that the worst possible situation is to be by yourself, because if there is no one else to interact with, you may have to experience yourself. And so you pull as many actors on your stage as you can to not be with yourself. But what might happen in the quietude of being with yourself is a contact and blending with the energies of which I am speaking. I would tell you, *you* are the best friend that you will ever have. In the presence of your true Self, you will become the most peaceful, the most relaxed, the most natural person possible. The one thing that you are running from is the one thing that can give you the peace that you are looking for. It

18

may be fun to be in an ashram, or go to lectures to be where people are, but when you go home it is all the same. Inner silence is where you will find yourself. You are running from the wrong thing. As always, the world is 'upside down.' You see the many, but there is only One. You run from Self, and Self is your only real Savior! You are looking for a Savior and you already have one. It is *you*.

THE GIFT OF SEXUAL ENERGY
25 September 1983
Albuquerque, New Mexico

In order to sensibly discuss the subject of sexuality, we will have to travel back in time. It will come as no surprise to you that sexuality is not a modern phenomenon and the problems that have arisen around it are ancient, varied, and very exotic. To gain a vaster perspective, we will look at what your sexual obligations are. I am not here to lay down 'laws' for sexual behavior. You are responsible for this, just as you are responsible for every law under which you operate.

So, to travel back, we come to a time, past time as you know it, when your species came to the earth plane, took form, and decided what it wanted to do. At that time you were given 'powers.' The powers you were given are those energies which you relate to the seven chakras. You have now come to see the energies moving in certain organized patterns, but the powers I am referring to move constantly through your Being and were designed to do certain things. One of them is to think, and one is to feel. When we speak of sexual energy, we are speaking of one of these powers. You were given this power and this energy to be used as you each, individually, chose to use it. In the beginning, it was not at all separated from the other bands of energy; there was not much difference between the drive that impelled you to go out and hunt your prey, and the drive that impelled you toward a sexual relationship. There was not, in the beginning, much differentiation.

When the energies moved through all of you many lifetimes ago, each one of you made your own choices, choices that seemed in harmony with who you were and who you wanted to be. Please understand that this lifetime is not your first experience on this planet. You have been on a journey for a very long time. So you have come with certain built-in tendencies from other lifetimes which are outpictured through your own being, your own consciousness. These tendencies have produced certain attitudes in you toward sexuality and have become a part of who you are. As you moved through time and space, this energy became a part of your expression and you did with it whatever you willed to do. Sexual energy, like all of the other energies, was meant to be a *personal* responsibility. It was to be a part of your Beingness of which you could be acutely aware. You were intended to experience your *own* rightness of feeling and action.

By observation, you learned that your thoughts can bring harmony or disharmony into your life, and you are responsible for what you think. So also are you responsible for how you use your sexual energy. But the days of acknowledging those responsibilities are long gone. Man has constructed codes of behavior on every level of consciousness and you no longer accept your own responsibility. You go to the law, to your rules to tell you what to do, and you think in that way that you can avoid responsibility. Has it worked? Have the sexual codes laid down in the 'dark ages' (under which you are still operating) given you fulfillment? I would suggest that you become aware of your own sexuality, claim your own reality; do the things that make *you* feel creative, dynamic, alive, loving, positive, exciting, excited. This is your responsibility! If you look to a 'code' to tell you what to do, you will end up being conflicted in your desires. You believe that God cares, in the most minute detail, what you do with your sexuality. But He doesn't care. That is *your* business. He does not care any more than your neighbor should care. He has only one concern, and that is the quality of your awareness, your power, your love, and your compassion. If you have been following the rules and find yourself being angry, negative, resentful, or judgmental, do not think that you are in harmony with the Divine.

The issue of sexuality often comes up and I always find the same dilemma presented: If you all started to do what *you* wanted to do sexually, what would the world be like? If you take away all the rules, what will happen? The answer to this is where you and I part company. I have absolute confidence that if you were to drop your outer rules, you would find your own inner rules to be so much more humane, spontaneous, loving, and kind. I believe in you where you do not believe in yourself. You seem to think that you are like caged animals, and that if the cage were opened, the rules gone, you would become some kind of sexual beast. My friends, it is not like that. You are a part of the Createdness that carries with it an awareness of what is most beneficial should *you* choose to do it. But when you turn to a rule instead of to yourself, things become unclear. The law within your own being is absolutely predictable. I know that, because I know the Law upon which you rest. Do you not realize that you did not create yourself? You are a 'given' Creation! You have been given the wonder of *you*. There *is* a Law within you that you did not create, and which is absolutely dependable. It is much more dependable than any law that man has ever made. When you decide to trust your own Being, you will find there all the virtues that you have been seeking—compassion, understanding, harmony, courage, wisdom, all! Your own nature, your essence of Being, is part of the Source. Where do you think this 'raw material' came from in the first place? In the moment of your creation, you were given incredible gifts; and one of the most important is the gift of sexuality!

You become confused when you move out into the world. You have certain feelings and emotions that you try to harmonize with other people. You have different opinions; you are different. If you wish to understand sexuality, do not view it with your thinking mind. You learn lessons from that Power *when it is in motion*. The energy itself is as pure as any energy that you could possibly imagine. The perversion comes in your mind. The Power rises, and the mind then takes over and makes judgments as to 'right' and 'wrong.' Ask yourself what purpose you use sexuality for. Some of you use your sexual power to manipulate other people; you become very 'good'

at it, and use it to control, and some of you use your sexual power to punish other people; you become very 'bad' at it, and use it to control. Some of you don't use it at all.

If any power were to be placed in your hands, you would ask what to do with it, whom to share it with, how to affect your life with it. You cannot see your sexuality, but you can feel it as power within you and so you must ask these questions of yourself. What do you wish to use your sexuality for? That is an individual question which must be answered by each one of you in the deepest part of your Being. Do not be afraid to address that question, you will not become the wild animal that you fear. What you will find through a deep probing into the issue is the greatest *ally* the physical body has. You use 'allies' from the so-called spirit world but I am talking about an ally that is right here. Sexuality is your ally because it gives you an opportunity to better understand yourself through being part of your own naturalness. And it takes a great deal of courage to become introspective enough to look at that area with honesty. Any one, no matter what their age, who has feelings of sexuality that are in some way distorted, or physical desires that make them unhappy or uncomfortable, should recognize them as areas of 'unfinished business.' If you do not have sexual expression in your life, it is because *you* have decided that you did not want it. When sexual desire is expressed, if it is in line with your beliefs, it will find a match. If you are sitting on your sexual power because you think you are too ugly, or too fat, or too old, or for whatever reason, then that is the belief you project into the world, and that is what you will experience. Some feel that avoiding the sexual issue entirely will solve their dilemma, only to find that it keeps reappearing. People sometimes have operations so that they will not have to deal with their sexuality, only to find that the energy is still present, still moving in their bodies. You are not going to get rid of the energy, for it is a part of the physical body. Sexuality can *always* be an ally because it is one of the strongest drives of the physical vehicle. Deal with it now, or deal with it next lifetime, but you will eventually have to face this issue. You need only clarify how you are going to use this great gift, and when you do, your life will begin to change. You will find that many of your experiences will be different. Things will enter your life that had not been present, and things will leave your life that have been in it. Your responsibility is to ask and answer the question—What do I wish to use this amazing power for?

I would like to be outrageous enough to suggest what might have been the Divine hope with regard to this power. Let us use an analogy. You have a teenager, and it comes time to give him or her a car—perhaps a Porsche, a wonderful and beautiful car. And as you present the keys, you are thinking, "Oh my God, oh my God!" because there is the awareness that incredible power can be used to take incredible chances and the teenager is so young. And so, when the Divine gifts of Power were bestowed, there was also a ringing in the consciousness, "Oh my God!" The hope was that the power might be used in different, conscious ways. One was for your pleasure! For the sheer wonder and pleasure of it. Another was to give you an awareness that power *is*, that it exists, and it moves, it creates, takes form, is dynamic and changeable. Can you think of any power, besides the power of your mind, that has that capacity? And finally, a higher use for this gift. There is gratitude, great gratitude for the physical pleasure, and gratitude for the feeling of being alive, of being more, more than the physical body. But after experiencing the pleasure, and the aliveness and the wonder of the feeling as it comes in from outside, and fills and moves you, is it not possible to see that same power as being reversible? Let me explain. You now feel sexual energy as coming to you, or arising within you. The hope was that one day you might see that it could also move in the other direction so that you could 'ride' that power back to the Source from which it came. Energy moves both ways, so if you could 'ride' it back, you would be connected with the Source from which that energy came!

There are many ways to do that, and there are no rules to riding that bridge back. The difficulty is that you all believe there are. You have all read the 'right' books, had the teachers, and have followed the 'right' path. Those of you who have had even a glimpse of the bridge now find yourself in a dilemma. And it has to do with your belief systems. Now you feel you are not *qualified* to ride that bridge back, or that in order to cross that bridge, you have to pay a toll. Therefore, you do not pay attention to the lessons that the sexual energy is trying to teach you every moment of your sexual experience. You 'leave'; you do not stay in that experience. Many things distract you. Guilt comes in; you feel that you should not be doing it, and you hope that God is not watching, or that your teacher is not watching. So you are 'not there,' you go on semi-automatic, and you fail to feel the wonder and the movement. Sexual energy is an ally, but no ally, no matter how powerful, can help you if you are not there, if you are not listening. You must be there, paying attention to everything that is going on, to your responses, your feelings, how the energy moves, how it liberates, where it is stuck, and what to do with it. If you are not there, you are lost and you have lost the teaching.

When you are not happy in your sexual life, many of you think that the answer is to add more people to your experience. Then, if you still have any energy left, you realize that you are still not happy— but have added a lot more trouble to your life, for now you have more egos to keep satisfied! Or you may decide that the trouble is with your present partner, that if you found a more sensual person you would be happy. So you find another partner only to discover that you still feel unfulfilled. Sexual energy will fulfill you only when it is used wisely on all levels. Anything short of that and you will remain unsatisfied because the energy was never meant to stop at any level of gratification.

How then, to open to these deeper experiences? Just as some of you sit in meditation, very aware of the energy patterns as they move through you, thereby learning that these energies are not of the limited self, so will the awareness of sexual energy bring you in touch with its 'triggering effect.' If you wish to use your sexual expression in such a way that it will nourish you on all levels, you will have to listen, and pay attention to what is happening inside and around you. You will have to become very quiet and very intense. You will need to be *aware*, and you will have to feel and come to know the movement of that energy. With observation, you will find that the genital area is very close to the trigger point of the kundalini. When your awareness is totally present, you will find that you have the ability to 'pull the power up' and to raise it from your lower chakra to your highest, igniting them all along the way.

If you do not feel the wonder of that power, it is because something in your mind has asked you to turn it off. Please understand that this energy does not flow in one direction only. You cannot separate, in a 'rod of power,' one end from the other, for they are joined. Sexuality is God's gift to you, and every gift that is given has been given for one main reason. It is to be used eventually for the journey 'home', to be used to come back to the Source. The teenager can take the car and the money, and do whatever he wants, but the parents hope he will eventually use them to drive home. It is no different with God. He allows you to go and play, and do all those wonderful things that you and the teenagers do; but eventually He hopes you will begin to realize that you are lonely and want to go 'home'. Do with the energy what you will, in whatever way you want, in whatever lifetime; but understand, it was given so that you could use it to make your way 'home'!

Are there any questions?

Q: I have understood that the 'kundalini' as power could be very dangerous, and to seek it one should have a teacher. Is this true?

If you are going to use various spiritual disciples such as long meditation, austerities, pranayama, etc., in order to 'get' this kundalini power, and insist that it rise at your command, then you will need a guide. Speaking from my own incarnative pattern, I can tell you that I did not have a guide, that I had no one around who had the slightest intimation of what I was trying to do. All I had was the movement of the energy itself. And I will tell you that it was absolutely reliable, it moved in its own way, in its own good time and it did not take me too fast, or too far, and everything was *all right*. When you let the energy lead the way, moving as it will, it creates its own pathway. It is like a small stream moving freely down a mountain. But if you break open a dam and release the energy all at once, the rush could be dangerous. Let it happen in its own good and wondrous time. Do not think that you need to have a teacher for everything. The teacher is *you*! That power is within you, and you do have a regulatory system. As the energy moves, it will clear the way. Do not take my word for it—but do not take anyone else's either; play fair and listen to yourself. Once you try it, you will find that you *do* know something about your own energy, and you will not have to feel separated from you sexuality any more.

The purpose of sexual union is to nourish you on all levels. If you have a partner who is also interested in sexual understanding, I would suggest that you begin along these lines to investigate the source of that nourishment. Some of you may want to buy some books on Tantric Yoga, but you do not *need* to do that. Write your own book about *your own* sexual understanding. You be the laboratory and the subject. Let us suppose that you are at a party. Someone comes up to you, and you feel the sexual energy begin to rise. The disciplined one would at once ask, "Would it be useful to experience this energy now?" If you are on the lowest level of expression, the usefulness is obvious. Pleasure. So you go and do, or don't, as you choose. If you are on a higher level (I mistrust 'levels,' but aren't we having fun!), then you can say, "I will have to think about it, for to activate this now would create more chaos in my life, and it may or may not be worth it." If you decide it is worth it, then do it, if not, then don't and be prepared to accept the responsibility of your action. At the highest level you might ask, "Would this expression, under these circumstances, with this person, be maximum in my reaching Divine understanding or not?" In the end, you will learn something that you might not want to know; like attracts like. If you are on the lowest level only, it is unlikely that you will be attracted to someone on a higher level, for they will appear lacking in spontaneity to you. One step up is where you find the 'committed lovers,' who are not necessarily committed to higher awareness, but to each other. On the highest level you will find only those who are seeking to use everything in their universe to come Home.

Q: How does one move this energy?

Locate the power in a specific part of your body, then deepen your awareness of it by *staying with it*. Since you know that thought creates, you can consciously decide that you are going to bring it up through your body and so it begins to move. You do not have only seven chakras, as most of you tend to believe. There are many chakras located all over the body. When you begin to move the energy, these centers trigger each other to 'light up.' It is a movement in the synapses, and it is very rapid movement over which you have little control once it begins. Your job is to be aware of the energy, concentrate on it and your desire to move it up. Then allow it to move. The moment that you put your awareness on any area of your physical body, the energy will move there, so start with the lowest chakra and concentrate in turn on each of the others. This will move the energy up through and out of the crown chakra. Try it. And remember, this is one of the greatest gifts that you have been given! There were no rules made along with the gift; you have made them all for yourself. Just as you are responsible for the quality of your speech, for the quality of your actions, for the quality of everything in your life, so also are you responsible for the quality of your sexual activities. It is up to you. There is no 'wrong' and there is no 'right'; there is simply choice!

Q: Do we make rules around sexuality because we are afraid to go 'home'?

Sexual rules were made by people who did not feel free in their sexual expression. I am not talking about this modern age, but about the priests of old. They set themselves apart and decided that sex was an activity in which they should not indulge. The minute this rule was made it was imposed on others. When this happened, it became obvious that sexuality would end up with many restrictions. The rules were adhered to, even in the face of the fact that many people have become totally enlightened during the sexual union. The priests felt that if you did not Awaken by following the rules, then your experience was not valid, just like the prevalent medical belief that if you are healed by other than medical rules, there must have been a mistake in the original diagnosis. If you are following the religious rules, then credence is given to your 'enlightening' experience. Please do not believe that it was God who made the rules you follow. God does not *make* you do anything; and I tell you that much of what is going on is an *experiment*. Life is dynamic action in creation. What would be the point of God laying it all out, and then you playing it according to a script? Life is an amazingly wonder-filled creation that is on-going, and you are part of it. And all that you think and say and do is a part of it. There are no 'mistakes'; there is nothing 'wrong.' It is all Life.

And I have yelled long enough. Thank you all for coming.

THE LOVE OF SELF
26 February 1984
Albuquerque, New Mexico

Before we began this morning, I was asked: If life is a learning process, why does it have to be so painful? I would like to see if I can weave the question as well as the answer into a tapestry of meaning.

There is a very poignant point to this question. If it is true that you came to this earth plane to learn, then why does it appear to be so difficult? If it is supposed to be a life of moving spontaneity, wonder, and beauty, then why does it so often appear other than that?

We have been spinning some grand theories here—cosmological facts, hopes, and desires, but in the end my friends, we have to come to one basic reality. There come moments in your life when you realize that you have only one thing, and that is yourself. All of the 'props' that you use during a lifetime to make yourself feel at ease in the world will eventually fail. If you have been in relationship with others who have fed meaning into your life, someday you will awaken and find yourself alone. If you have children, they grow up; if you have an important position in life, you retire or it is taken from you; if you have beauty, you become old; if you are powerful, you become weak and infirm.

Many come to me and say, "I want, more than anything, to know God." And what they want to know is how they can get rid of all the things that they 'know' God does not love about them. How to get rid of 'negative' emotions such as anger or jealousy. But how do you get rid of something that is a part of you? Many creative ways are tried. The first way usually attempted is to withdraw from all the situations and people that can cause anger and never enter into relationships which can cause jealousy. And since those emotions make you feel less than you want to be, you constrict your life to rid yourself of them. In extreme cases, constriction leads to 'renunciation,' and whether you sit in a cave or your house, the desire is to cut off all stimulation that might provoke those reactions you are trying not to feel. But comes the day when you leave the house or come down off the mountain and go to your neighborhood store. Someone pushes into line in front of you and your peaceful interior explodes into anger. When you finally realize that renunciation is not working, the next attempt is to *will* yourself not to be angry. Then your face becomes a mask. A smile is fixed there and the jaw is rigid. You have to keep smiling, because if you start to relax you might cry, you might scream, or you might do something else 'inappropriate.' You try, by your will, to override the emotions that are moving through you. And this works for a while, until one day an unsettling event occurs and before your jaw can clench, you respond with the same feelings and the same fears that you are trying to overcome. What have you accomplished?

Concurrent with all *these* maneuvers, you are playing the wonderful game of manipulation. You manipulate the people in your universe so they will not bother you, for if *they* are behaving, you will not have to misbehave. If your lover is very clear about not making you jealous, you will not feel jealousy; if you pick a boss that never gets angry, you don't have to deal with anger. So, you manipulate your environment. You leave behind the things that are too hard for you to deal with, because you don't want to face that part of yourself. You move from one relationship to another trying to find someone who will be a passive mirror for you, so that you do not have to see those 'negative' aspects of yourself. But in the last, it all fails. You are left, one day, sitting with the understanding that you cannot, on your own, rid yourself of the little 'demons' that run around in you. And so comes another brilliant idea—you'll let God do it! You can't do it, so you will let God do it for you. Now, you have to *find* Him first and then ask Him to take all these unpleasantries away for you. Haven't you all tried asking Him to do this at one time or other? Has anything changed? So now comes the wonderful game of 'spiritual awakening,' and you begin a long process toward 'enlightenment.' You go to the teacher and read all the 'right' books, do all the 'right' things, chant all the 'right' mantras, are very intense and are *so* good. And at the end of this process you hope to find God and be free from your negative side.

At this point, I would like to digress from our discussion a moment. Many of you who know Mary-Margaret well, no doubt have asked, "Why was *she* picked for this job?" There is a reason which she probably doesn't even remember. As a young girl living on a small island in the Pacific, she spent many hours alone and would go to an old Hawaiian church and sit on the rubble and swing her feet and ponder. It occurred to her that she was in a community filled with diversified religions that she needed to make sense out of if she was to fit in. Hawaii has, among others, Buddhists, Mormons, Catholics, Zen Buddhists, Christians, and the original Hawaiians with their Kahuna doctrines. This young girl attended these different churches because her father was in a position where he had to go, and he would take her with him. In time, a great deal of diversified material was placed in her consciousness and she pondered on how to reconcile the tremendous differences that were truly obvious to her. So she sat there, swinging her feet and wondering. Then out of her Awareness came the conviction (not an idea) that in order to reconcile this dilemma, she must answer the following: how can a person, alone on an island, with no books, no friends, nothing but himself or herself, find God? This became the basis for her search. And what I have to say today is the answer to the question that she presented to herself those many years ago—for in the end, you *are* one person on an island, and all the books you have read and the prayers you have prayed, in the face of your emptiness, have no meaning.

So please begin by accepting the fact that the basic who-ness of you will probably not change very much. No matter what you do, or what kind of mental gymnastics you might perform, you will pretty much remain yourself. *You are who you are*, the end product of billions of experiences. So you begin by acknowledging that *you are who you are*. When you have made this statement deep within your being, and are presented with a feeling of jealousy for example, you can look around and see again that you are trapped. You are trapped because you cannot get away from the feeling of jealousy. You are not going to get away *because you don't have to*. Your life has been based on the supposition that there is something wrong with you that you've got to fix. I would like to suggest that there is nothing wrong with you, and you certainly don't need to be fixed. Your inner tension comes from *not loving* certain parts of yourself. And you don't love them because you have been told not to by people who are ignoring those parts of themselves they do not love. Your freedom comes from going within and saying with all the power of your being, "I love myself in the midst of jealousy. I love myself in the act of anger. I love myself when I feel self-pity." Whatever it may be, in the midst of that feeling, in the midst of that thought, in the midst of that action, your freedom lies in saying, "I love myself in this moment, just as it is."

I can see the fear in some of your minds that if you love that part of yourself, you will be stuck with it for the rest of your life. I would like at this point to give you a cosmological view of what really happens in and around you, and how these emotions arise and why acceptance is your way out. Please try and follow. The reality is this: thoughts are in motion around you at all times. Between you and these thoughts, there is something you call your 'aura.' Because of your individual tendencies, you choose certain thoughts as they go by, and draw them to you. You tend to pull in the same ones all the time, so you go down the same roads over and over again. Thoughts of unworthiness, of fear, of depression; depreciating, negative thoughts, again and again. Now, an important point. When the thought comes in, it translates itself inside your physical body as a feeling. The feeling comes into you and records itself

36

inside what you would call your soul. At that moment, a future action is formed. Do you understand the process? The thought is out there. It comes through your auric field. It hits you. It's recorded as a feeling. Out of that feeling within yourself, *you* formulate a future action. For example; a thought goes by: "That person doesn't like me." Anger is the feeling, and the future action is revenge.

You came to the earth plane to experience the full range of emotions and to become master of those emotions. Mastery comes by realizing that you can *choose* your responses, which thoughts you pull in and what actions you bring about in your life. And what I am suggesting to you today is that most of the thoughts that you pull in are based on the belief that there is something wrong with you, that you are not lovable, and that you have to do something in order to be loved. And I would like to reverse that process by asking you to begin a serious, ongoing commitment to the repetition of a mantra that has never occurred to you: *I love myself!* In an instant you can thereby go from despondency to happiness. Try it. Think of a happy thought and you will be blissful. Think of a depressing thought and you will move to unhappiness. And here you are, just sitting in a chair! Has anything happened to you? Has anybody hit you? Has anybody loved you? No! You're simply sitting, and you find that you have the capacity to move from 'high' to 'low.' And all you do is change your thought. You already know how to do this and you do it all the time. If it is true that you can sit quietly and change your mood in a moment, then perhaps it is also true that you can sit quietly and say with understanding, "I love myself," and begin to feel something happen inside your being. You will begin to feel a warmth. It is true that there is a 'flame,' a 'fire,' within. There is a chakra that 'lights up' through love. It is all true. By resting in that feeling of love for yourself, you begin to generate a warmth. I would ask you to try, for the next month, to give yourself some time every day to simply sit and feel this.

Now let us discuss what happens when a so-called negative

37

emotion arises. You are sitting there feeling warmth, feeling power, feeling wonderful, and the telephone rings. You pick it up and someone says, "You are a real jerk." Now a feeling enters that was not there a moment ago. The process is in motion, the thought goes by, you pull it in, and *you feel it*. Maybe it feels like a large, heavy, sharp rock. So you want to get rid of it. Your mind then starts the process of negating whatever statement came through, but in the end, it doesn't work. You've tried it before, and it hasn't helped.

What will work is this. The moment you sense that painful feeling within you, say to yourself, *"I love this feeling*. I welcome it. It doesn't have to go anywhere or change. It is a part of me. I accept this feeling." And the warmth which is always there, moves over to this 'rock' and begins to smooth it, surround it, and make it porous. So out of the power of your love for this 'rock,' 'it' takes on the power of your love. It becomes filled with your love! Love pours through this 'unlovely' feeling-mass, surrounds it, uplifts it, and it becomes 'lovely.' And you find you are capable of holding two things: *your love and that agony*. Your love is so vast that there is nothing that it will not hold, and using that vastness is what you've got to learn. No grief is so great that you cannot hold it within you and also hold the vast power of your love at the same time. You do not have to choose. You can have all the grief, you can have all the illness, you can have all the sorrow, all the regrets, all the guilt, and there is no need to worry because the love in your heart is so vast it will hold anything. These emotions are your children. *They are your children*! All they want is your love. You have created them, and then you treat them like bastards. But you created them! When you warm these emotions through your love of them, through your acceptance of them, then the words 'transmutation' and 'transformation' become real. Once you decide that you are so vast that you can hold anything, you will be fearless—fearless because you have learned there is nothing that can come to you from this world that you cannot hold. There is no grief so great, no event so horrible that you cannot hold it in you, smooth it, warm it, open to

38

it, and love it. Those of you who have had traumatic beginnings, don't run. Love them. Don't try to love the people, please. Love the feelings.

Organized religion (or even disorganized religion) would have you say that your job is to love your neighbor, but there's a little line that comes after that—as yourself. I would like to address this point. There is not one of you in this room that is not basically an entity who wants very much to love. And so when you're presented with the dilemma of having been hurt by someone and you want to love them but cannot because of the ache, you go through a lot of 'trying to love.' And that is honorable. The problem is that it doesn't work. And the reason it does not work is because you are asking yourself to do the hardest thing, which is to give something to someone that you want for yourself. *You* want love. And you are asking yourself to give it to someone whom your feelings tell you doesn't love you. I would like to suggest another position. Love yourself for not loving them. *Love yourself for not even liking them*! Understand, I'm not talking about a mental process, I am talking about an experiential *feeling*, and there is not one of you that cannot feel that warmth in the heart that I am talking about, if you would give yourself the chance. When you start to love yourself for *not* loving, or even for disliking someone, this wonderful alchemy begins, and the entire situation takes on a warmth, and you are no longer in a position of feeling badly because you can't love.

When you finally understand that *you* can generate that which you have been desperately looking for outside of yourself, you become the master of your life. You have been looking for love, security, and peace outside yourself, and the minute you find it inside yourself, you are the master. Not in the arrogant sense, but with a sense of wonder. Then you are in a position to love somebody else, and not before. Because until *that* moment, you are all asking each other for something, no matter how subtle you make it. And if they won't give it to you, then you're hurt, you're sad, you're lost, you're unloved, you're despondent. When mastery comes into your being, and you know that you love yourself, it isn't an *act* of love, it is *love in motion*. And you feel it, no matter who is before you, because then the love is not personalized. The dog goes by, the child goes by, the neighbor goes by, the enemy goes by, and *it is all the same*. It is frightening to think of loving the enemy as much as your own child, but when you become love in motion—*you are free*! When you have done for yourself what you have begged, pleaded, bartered, and manipulated the world to do for you, the game is over. No game remains because now you are Love in action, and everything you do comes from that state of abundance. It does not mean that you don't want to be with people, but it does mean you do not *need* to be with people. There is a difference. Out of the centered wonder of your own being you can be with others in a totally committed way. But not out of need—out of joy! Out of choice, not out of desperation.

As you sit with yourself and begin to say, "I love myself," there is going to arise a long list of things that you have judged as unlovable about yourself. "I would love myself if I wasn't a drug addict, or if I wasn't jealous, or if I didn't have a bad temper, or if I wasn't so fat, or so skinny." You have a long list that you may not even have thought about, and I suggest that you physically write out your list. Get it out there and then no matter how long it takes, reverse it. "I love myself *while* being a drug addict." I am talking about the willingness to love all the 'bastard' parts of yourself which you have not allowed yourself to love before. Many of you think you were 'conceived in sin,' and that from the very beginning there has been something wrong with you that you've got to figure out before you die. There is nothing wrong with you. What's 'wrong' are your thoughts, and that's all that has *ever* been wrong. You will never be free of these 'children,' and who wants to be? You do not want them living in your house when they're forty-five, you want them to be free, creative, dynamic, alive, and going about their business. But you don't want to be free of them. And these emotions are your 'children.' They make up the wonderful substance of you, of your creations, of who you are, and of who you have been—they are a part of you!

Again, religion would tell you that there are sins in the world that have to be overcome; but it is my experience that when you love your 'children' (emotions), you love *all* those parts of yourself that have been labeled sinful, that keep showing themselves year after year. You are going to be at this process until the day you die. And why not? Every day something new is born. You are a creative, dynamic, exploding wonder and you are going to change every day. Parts of your being are going to come forward daily and every new experience will show you a new face. You are going to find out things about yourself that you never dreamt possible. Some fears, some courageous powers, some humor, some laughter, some tears, some anger—it's all there in a beautiful ever-changing pattern, and *that is the wonder of it*! If you will stop trying to freeze the pattern into the perfect form, then *you can enjoy the movement of the parts*. You are trying to freeze yourself into a 'perfect form' based on an unreal idea of who Jesus Christ was, of who Buddha was, of who you think God wants you to be. You have even tried to freeze God into some form, and I tell you that He is smarter than that, and means to be ever moving, ever changing, ever evolving, ever extending, ever wondrously different. Otherwise, why bother? Do you really think God wants to sit around bored with Himself ad infinitum? What kind of a God would create all this, to have it always the same? This Power that spawned you in the beginning was brilliant! You didn't create yourself, but you are surely a part of it.

Because you have believed that unless you are perfect, you cannot have God's love in you, you believe you are not capable of love. *That is a lie*! Some of your parents have even said, "If you have sexual relations before you are married, God will not love you." And you believed it, but not well enough not to do it, just well enough to feel guilty about it. Your nature is such that it wants to experience, and parents want you *not* to experience! So you are in a paradoxical position from the beginning. The drama is set from the moment life begins, and the basic difficulty is in your believing the lie. I have told you that you did not create yourselves, but that out of the Source of all things, you came; and just as every child is a part of the parent, so are you a part of the Source, and there's no way to escape it. That Source is within you! When you say, "I love myself," you can feel a response because within your physical body there is an Essence, a Power, a Substance, a Light, that is there waiting to be kindled. Meditation for many of you has not kindled it because you have not loved yourselves. Each time you say, "I love myself," and are willing to feel that love, you are turning up the Power, fanning the Flame, letting the Light in. You do not have to go out and find the 'substance' of Love, because it is inside you. By turning your attention toward self-love, you ignite the *power* of your love. There is no more love in any one of you than there is in another, there is no less love. *There is no difference.*

Let's talk about this in terms of something simple like soup. You all have a bowl of soup in you. In the Christ's or the Buddha's case, it is an ignited, powerful, moving ambrosia. It has a wonderful aroma, and They can feel it because it is on fire and warms them, and it motivates their lives and gives them a strong sense of aliveness. So, *your* problem is that you have cold soup! And that is not a very large problem. Once you understand that your job is simply to turn up the fire, you will be your own Master—because you know exactly how to turn up your own fire. *You* know the things that make your life alive. *You* know the things that make your life feel worthwhile, the things that make you want to get up in the morning and go about your business. And you also know the things that make you want to stay in bed and pull the covers over your head. So, for God's sake, and I mean that literally, do the things that you want to do—things that ignite your life, give you power and a feeling of inner warmth. And stop doing the things that deaden you! The power within you that moves at your command, to love and embrace your 'children' within you, is the Love of God. Do not forget, you are That. You have always been That, you have never been anything other than a part of God, ever! And that Divinity, that everlasting Divinity is always there, moving at your command.

And when you will *it* to embrace your agony and your fear, it does. And it will hold them in an embrace of total acceptance, and in that embrace you will not be agonized any more. Do you think the Christ never cried? Do you think the Buddha never ached? You are not going to be less human, you are going to be wholly human. Because in your wholeness you will know that those emotions are you, but they are not all of you. In the amazing otherness of you, as mother and father to those children, you embrace them, hold them, and love them, and in that love you are one with them. You become one with yourself through your love of yourself and all of the parts of you. There is no other way home, because you are home, and the wholeness of you is waiting. You are *all* of it, so please stop trying to be less.

43

SELF

You become ignorant when you try to
understand things with your mind.

FEAR
8 September 1979
Albuquerque, New Mexico

Q: Would you speak on the subject of fear?

That dark and difficult side of the human movement toward Freedom that you choose to call 'fear,' is what I would choose to call *a lack of understanding*. I will say now: *there is nothing in the universe to fear!* The illusion that the dark mirror of the ego has presented to you distorts your view of life to such an extent that you believe that there is indeed something to fear. You look upon the fearful events of your life and search around in your mental or emotional bag to try and find what you call the 'remedy.' If you will pay attention, I think you will find that a series of events takes place. First you experience fear. Second, you experience the desire to remove yourself from this feeling of fear. Third, you go to your mind and look there to see if there is something there that you can find to remedy the 'illness.' Fourth, sometimes you find something that is a temporary expedient and you do it. This is where I would ask for your closest attention. If you have a fear that you have not truly overcome, watch very carefully and see if it is not replaced by another fear. Most people on the earth plane go through life moving from one fear to another. Each time they overcome a difficulty, they feel good and more secure about their life and they are confident again. Then life is normal, exciting and even joyful at times. But again at some point, another fearful spector will enter their life in a different form.

The reason that you do not uproot fear is that you have made one very important mistake. You think that fear has more than one root and that if you pull all of them out, you will come to a state in which you have no fear. But if you are being realistic, you will see that you have programmed yourself against such success, because in all honesty you know that some day you will have to face the ultimate fear, which is the fear of death. Do what you will about the problems between this moment and the moment of your death, but that point must come. Those of you who have worked deeply with the awareness of an oncoming death situation realize that the fear can be overcome. But those of you who have not, I can assure you that death will come to you in its own time. So I suggest that instead of taking small measures of expediency to remove fear in small increments, we make a broad and sweeping statement about fear, and so see it in its own raw awareness, and dispense with it once and for all.

How many of you believe me when I tell you that you can live a life totally without fear? God, the Almighty Source, did not program life for you to be filled with fear and trepidation and sickness unto death! That is *not* the Divine plan; that is *yours*, and you have all done a very good job of it. But now I would speak with those of you who are tired of such a situation and who would like to face life not with fear, but with boldness and vigor, courage, compassion and understanding. So, how do you come to an understanding of what you fear, and then to the ultimate question of how to uproot it?

Again I tell you, unless you take your life seriously, you are not going to be able to confront the ultimate fear within your being. When I say 'seriously' I do not mean soberly, with sadness, but with a serious mind. If you do so, then one of the things you must come across is that there are many things that agitate the surface of your mind. And they go in deep pools that eddy down into the darkness; a darkness that you do not wish to explore. With all due respect to psychologists, I would like to say that there is nothing to fear in that dark pool of the unconscious. Nothing! One of the modern fears is that in the unconscious reside frightful beings or monsters with long tentacles. These are figments of your own mind. What is really to be found in those deep recesses is *your own divinity*; nothing else. Below the agitation, in the depths of the water, lies the Source, the Source from which you spring and there is nothing to fear. You have created your fears and why do you fear what you have created? Please face the fact that the demons of your life are created by you, for then you will have the courage to face them. What you create, you are willing to face. As long as you put the power of the creation onto some god outside yourself, you are afraid to look. If you say that your 'devils' come from another source and are unknown to you, they will be beyond your capabilities to handle and you will no longer be courageous. No God created your devils, so get about the business of looking. When you decide that you do not wish to live with fear any more, fear of any kind, of any sort, and for any reason, I assure you that you will be given the strength to face what it is that you so fear to see. And it is not very difficult. If you are sincere about Freedom, then I ask you to look within to find where your fears lie. They will not elude you. In fact, when you are paying attention, you will find that they start to surface in many ways. You will find them in books, in dreams, on the lips of other people, and in the form of your own fantasies as you go about your day. They will clearly present themselves to you and you will not need to go very far to find them.

Please be aware that this is *a benevolent universe*. It is on *your* side and when you decide to join the universal harmony instead of remaining in your own personal disharmony, all of the forces of the Universe will move in to help you, because it is their desire to have you as a co-participant, not isolated and encapsulated in your own private hell. Your own private hell is something that you have created. And you live isolated within it, continually going into the same areas of awareness and pulling out the same darkness, the same fears, the same misunderstandings and bringing them before your mind's eye, again and yet again. These are your devils. Do not be too arrogant about the 'dynamic' creations of your own ego because ego boundaries do not extend very far. They are not upheld by the dynamic, eternal energy of the Divine, thus, they have only limited life-span and limited power. When you become serious about introspection, Divine Power begins to come into your life to remove these fears from your mind.

Let us be very specific. Let us say that you have an overwhelming fear of being abandoned, of being left alone. There are several ways in which you can deal with this. If you try a therapist, please go to the one that you feel has the best spiritual understanding, not necessarily the highest degree from the finest university. It is the depth of the therapist's intuitive faculty that will help release those secrets that are impinging upon that moment. For often it does lie in a past, incarnative situation and that a very attuned therapist can help you understand it. But let us say that you do not have vast amounts of money or that you are not in a position to find such an enlightened therapist. Therefore you are left with only yourself. I feel that this ultimately may be the best situation. In that moment, you have yourself, your problem, and your determination to become clear of this problem, so you have the three necessary components to reveal the answer. That is *all* that is needed. And please never forget, *with the problem is the answer*. You have programmed these things linearly: now is the problem, and tomorrow has the answer. That is not reality. Now is the problem, and *now* is the answer unless you choose to prolong your agony because you desire the emotional feeling associated with being involved in problems. Understand my friends, most of you adore your problems. They give you a great deal of emotional satisfaction because they make you feel alive, dynamic, creative, charged with energy. This is one way to enjoy life—may I suggest another. If you would put aside your problems for just a small amount of time and instead spend that time tapping into and becoming one with Divine Energy, you would be so filled with creative power that you would see the pale comparison and never again would you forget. You are so transfixed by your problems and your desire to solve the thousand psychological dilemmas of your lifetime, that you do not see the real question or hear the real answer. *How can you be free?* How can you be free from all the limitations the ego places on the psyche by filling it with illusions? How can you be free *now*, for all time, from fear. Fear is the human condition. It is not found in other areas of awareness. It is your creation, your created consciousness and as such must be faced here in order to overcome it. You have created it, and it is in this area of consciousness that you must remove it. How then to do this?

When you feel fear, you feel it as a physical thing—which is what it is. Many times it is felt as a constriction in the chest, throat, or head. Instead of following whatever unsuccessful ritual you usually try, try something else. I would suggest the following: first, allow the movement of that fear to play upon the physical form in any way it wishes. Do not try to remove it, to turn it, to swallow it, or get away from it. Be in a totally receptive state and allow it to move. *Allowance* is the first step. If you pay attention, you will see that it comes in waves. Fear is not an on-going power because it is not divinely motivated. And be grateful that this is so, for now you know that there is a way to end your difficulty. So first, allow the fear to play upon you.

Second, when you feel the troughs between the waves of your fear, I would suggest that, very carefully, you stay centered in the awareness that fear is present. Please do not say "I am afraid." The statement should be "Fear is present." There is a great deal of difference between those two statements. And at that time center yourself as deeply as you can in the area of the heart. Center yourself with all the determined will that you can muster, and sit there. Simply sit there. Interesting things will begin to happen if you are absolutely determined to observe the emotion of fear. The more time you spend centered in this area, the greater your power will be when you are in difficulty. So make the most use of the days when you are free of fear, for there will come times when you will need to be centered. You cannot call upon Peace if you have not practiced it. You cannot call upon Universal Love if you have not wished for it. It does not come only on your command; it comes when you build the power daily. As you sit there quietly within this awareness, as you feel the movements within, you will see that the heart center is where all fear fades. When you become serious about facing your fears, you will find more and more of your days and nights filled with a dynamic quality that frees you from your own illusory creation. Man calls this quality Love. It is the power within the center of the heart that allows you to know your connectedness with everything and everyone. There is nothing outside of you, all is within, and there is nothing to fear. If you doubt me, I would ask you to give me one year of your time when you practice this as many moments of your days, your evenings and your nights as you can. I will promise you this: the unconditional love that you seek lies quietly waiting within the center of your being and once you have tapped into it, you will never, ever, fear again. It is truly spoken that Love fears nothing. The reason that it fears nothing is that It knows that all but Itself is illusion. If you doubt me, and I see every reason that you should, accept the challenge and try it! Spend as many moments of your days as you can, quietly resting in the center of your being, not allowing your fears to pull you away and *you will experience what we are talking about.*

Q: What do I do with my fear of physical pain?

So then my friend, you think you are a body. But you are more than a body. It is possible to live without fear of *any* kind. And to reach that kind of awareness means that you have to go to the ultimate point, where you see clearly that you are *not just a body.* If you look at the things you fear, you will see that almost all of them are connected with the idea that you are a body. If you were a body there would be many reasons to fear, but if you can see that you are not, certain other possibilities open up. If you are trapped in the belief that you are just a body, you will suffer, you will die, you will be left, you will be abandoned, you will starve, you will be too hot, you will be too cold, you will not get what you want, you will be given what you don't want and on and on and on. The ultimate destruction of this fear lies in the kernel of knowledge that "Thou are not that." And you say, what about the body that is riddled with disease, and the pain that is overwhelming?

When there is pain, the body has certain physical reactions that are natural to it. What happens to those who are in a state of Awareness is that they observe with great equanimity that pain is present. They are not involved in the pain but they acknowledge that there is pain. The illusion here is the idea that thou art that body. This is why I have to play my old record again. When you take time each day to meditate, you can free yourself from the body illusion. It is through deep meditation that you will be lifted out of body form; either expanded out or lifted totally out of it, as in an astral situation, so that you see that you are not that. Or, what is perhaps more common is to see with your inner eyes the body completely dissolved into something entirely different. It is not very helpful to say, "I am not the body; I am not the body." It is the truth, but just giving lip service to deep truth is not going to bring it any closer to your consciousness. If you wish to be free, you must go to the area within you that is most capable of expediting your freedom. And that is the space within. If you sit in your meditative state with what I call 'Divine solemnity,' wanting this to be revealed to you, it will be revealed to you. Again I say, *this is a benevolent universe*. When a child comes to his parent and says, "I am ready now to learn," does the parent say, "No, my child, come back in ten years." Of course not. The parent says, "By all means; sit down and let us begin." If you as parents can do this, cannot the Divine Powers do it also? Never underestimate the desire of the Divine to be unified. When your will is to be unified with the Divine, then know that you are in harmony with the Divine and all of its powers will come to your aid. But if you opt for diversity, separation, and isolation, then you must operate on your own, because the Divine will not rush to separate; it only rushes to unite. When you decide to lay fear aside, it will move for you.

When you speak of 'fear' of pain, you are speaking of an imagined future event, based on a past experience, and you are caught between two points (past and future) that do not exist. Indeed, you are overlooking the only point that does exist, which is the *now*. There is only one place where you can connect with the Divine

Power, and that is right now. What you think about, you will manifest. What you think about, you *must* manifest. Those of you who are exalting your despondency, who feel very put-upon by life, know that you are making your own misery. If you want to know why your world is as it is, spend some time observing your own thoughts and see. It will clarify much for you. If you are really perplexed about why your life contains so much chaos, why you can't see clearly, why you see alternatives but cannot choose, pay attention to what you think and you will see that your mind is giving energy to many areas, thus creating many possible realities. Energy follows thought. That is a Divine Law.

It is true that what you give the most attention to will end up with the greatest power. But fear takes a very subtle form. Let us say that you are afraid of this devil called cancer, that you are imbued with the fear that some day you will develop this illness and succumb. But there is another part of you that wants to manifest the radiant fullness of the compassionate One God. Whichever one of these appears in your life is the one to which you have given the most energy. If you wish, you may create any kind of horror for yourself. But you can also create the highest freedom for yourself. My job is to tell you that Freedom is possible; and to ask you to take it seriously, and to implant in your mind the remembrance of your desire for Freedom. I cannot free you, but I can tell you that it is possible, and you can do it. If you want to! And if you do not want to, then do not go to the feet of God and complain. It is *your choice.* When you realize that this is true and you finally take the responsibility for your own liberation, then you can be liberated. As long as you wait for 'Big Daddy God' to do it for you, you will wait until you die, because that is not His job. You created your limitations and you must destroy them. It is easily done. But the problem is, my friends, you love your limitations and want to keep them. They give meaning to your life. Where would you be if you had no problems? What would you do with your life, *if you had no problems?* Please think deeply about this. If you look carefully at the structure of your mind, you will see that you take meaning from solving your problems. But instead of solving them and being grateful, you say, "I must have another problem." You will find another problem. If it is not real, you will create one. If it is not banging upon your door, you will go out and borrow someone elses. You keep telling each other that you are filled with problems. You base communication and relationships on solving each other's problems. You may continue to hold that point of view, but understand it is not going to free you. I would challenge you to try living the next month believing that you had no problems. Watch the resistance that your ego puts up. Watch the power of the desire to solve either your own problems or someone else's. And realize that as long as you are dedicated to a problem solving proposition, you will never rise above it. This is why there are so many seekers and so few finders.

If you can lay aside your belief that solving problems is maximum, what will happen is that you will become filled with a vibrational frequency of such quality that, not only will it heal any disharmony within yourself, but it will be capable of extending itself to others to heal their disharmonies. If you wish to really perform a Divine service, I would ask you to give up worrying about your "non-existent" problems, allow your life to continue in whatever way it wishes and put your awareness where it will free you, deeply within your center. No matter how you may resent what I say, no matter how deeply you are committed to the difficulty of your own problems, I must tell you, there are none. And the moment you decide to see a world filled with Love and Light, with no problems, it will begin to manifest. And when it does, other people will not like it when you tell them their problems are not important. How then can you help?

Simply by being that which you are. And *your beingness* will take care of the 'problems.' You are mirrors, one to the other. What do you choose to mirror? Now as you mirror each others' problems, you are completely reinforcing the idea that you are limited. You look into each others' faces to see your own. That is where you see yourself. If you can move into an inner harmony and begin to radiate out a different face, it will truly be a different face! If you can begin to radiate this different face, then all who come and look upon you will be filled with hope—the hope of their own ultimate Freedom. If you wish to serve, then clear your own mirror, so that others will see nothing but their Divine Self. If you really want to help, quit the talking, quit the thinking, and begin the loving. Because it is in the power of unconditional loving that you see that there is nothing to fear. *Power and Love are one* . You know this. Thou art Love. That is what you experience, and that is what is true. It is what you are now, have always been, and always will be. Any mirror that shows you other than that is not reflecting truth. Please believe me! The ultimate ache is that you do not see that you are loved. As long as you look outside for love, you will never find it. The only love that is complete is that which comes from within, because it touches upon and is one with the everlasting Love that can never change. Human love, my friends, is still very capricious and part of you knows this, deeply. Will you seek something different?

Q: Are there human minds that have eliminated all traces of fear?

Yes, though it is rare. Once you have seen through the illusion, rarely do you return to the earth plane. Once the game has been called, once the separation is healed, there is no need to return, but you may choose to return in the form of a servant, a Bodhisattva, an Avatar, or an Enlightened One. So, looking around at the earth, we could observe a great deal of fear, but it is also true that many gain the knowledge that fear is self-created and has no meaning, therefore they leave. So there is all hope. It can be done. And I ask you to try. When you pass out of the body, at the time you call death, oftentimes clarity comes around the illusion of separation. But I would not wait until then, my friends, for I feel if you will try sincerely, that clarity is possible now. I would not be such a cruel, brother to come to you and tell you it is possible, but *you* can't do it!

56

I would not give you a preview of paradise and then tell you that you cannot enter. It is always possible, *now*!

Q: Are Love and the Now the same thing?

Yes. And why? Because Now and Love and the Divine are One. There is no separation between the Divine and the Now and the Love. Now exists, Love exists, and the Divine is here!

Q: Is there any way that we can really understand that 'there are no problems?'

If one is delighted with the idea of 'solving problems,' there is not much that can be done. But if you are immersed in a problem that is causing you such constriction and such pain that you have made the decision to die in the attempt to solve it, then you can pull away from it. If it is only inconvenient, then you will continue to be inconvenienced. If you wish a technique, the best one I can recommend is to *pay attention to what is really happening in your mind*. And if, after an honest survey of your thoughts for two weeks, you still want to continue to grind out the same petty thoughts, then we have nothing to say. But if you will honestly survey with deep awareness, your own thought patterns, you will see yourself hurting others, sending venomous thoughts to others, destroying their happiness, and wishing them ill. If you are being honest with yourself and not too holy, you will see trend of human thoughts. Human thought is divisive. It sees others as an attack upon itself, and therefore has to defend itself and defends itself in any way it can. As long as you believe you are being attacked, you will continue to defend yourself to the end of time. What are you putting out into the universe that you call your home? If you look within yourself for two weeks, and find that your only thoughts are loving ones, then we have nothing to say—you are consciously in the hands of your Inner Teacher and you are on your way to Freedom.

SPIRITUAL BEINGS ON THE EARTH PLANE
10 January 1982
Taos, New Mexico

Q: Would you speak to us on what it means to be a spiritual person?

The true hallmark of a spiritual person is one who has understood that there is so much wonder, so much mystery, and so much life that is totally beyond the realm of finite understanding that they have fallen into a space of gratitude and joy and acceptance.

The difficulty with defining yourself as a 'spiritual person' is that you immediately make a list of what a spiritual person does and does not do. Then you spend years trying to cram yourself into that definition. That is wonderful in the end, because if you go through this process long enough, you finally come to the understanding that you have not been able to do those things you have defined as spiritual. Yes, there are times when you are loving and compassionate, but there are also times when you are angry and resentful. Sometimes you are filled with self-pity, and sometimes you feel bold, strong and powerful. The lesson that you learn as you move through all of these different phases of your unfoldment should culminate at the point that tells you it is beyond your ability to understand what a spiritual person *really* is. And the minute you grasp that you cannot understand this with your mind, you fall into two things: compassion and hopelessness.

Compassion, because you realize that no one can totally understand and overcome their problems, so what gives you the right to judge against anyone? Compassion also, because you see how impossible it is to expect others to always be wonderfully balanced, when you cannot. At the same time, there is total hopelessness. Long ago, I said I liked the state of hopelessness and this is why. When I say hopeless, I do not mean a person who is desperate and filled with despair. The hopelessness I see is in the person who has finally surrendered to the basic knowledge that he or she cannot 'understand' life. You give yourselves headaches trying to 'understand.' When someone hurts you, you worry endlessly, wondering if it is the karma you have accrued from being abusive to others in past lives. How do you know, and why do you care? Does it really help you inside to know that you have gone through lifetimes of difficulty with other people? I don't think, in the last, that it eases the pain in your heart. Your head perhaps hurts a little less, because your mind can use the past to excuse your actions in the present. But does this really make you feel better? The minute the mind thinks it understands something, it rationalizes the action and forgets about it, so you never have to deal with it again.

My friends, if you will be very honest with yourselves, you will admit that again and again people hurt you. If you really understood one basic statement within your heart, you would never have to worry about people hurting you again. And the statement is this: Everyone in your world, everyone in the entirety of the world, is seeking *peace of heart*. You can aid in their search and your own by realizing that when they or you hurt another it is not deliberate. Do you understand that basically no one ever *means* to hurt anyone? Inflicting pain is not done out of hatred, with venom and remorse, it is done out of ignorance and fear. You become ignorant when you try to understand things with your mind. You look at someone and try to make sense of your relationship with them. You try with your children and with your parents, all the time telling yourself you must be able to understand, for then you will not hurt. Please hear one thing—*you cannot understand with the mind*. It is not that simple. *You* are not as simple as you would like to think. I keep telling you that you are incredibly Vast. If you are that Vastness, will you explain to me how your little mind can understand why you are doing what you are doing in your life, and why others do as they do? You keep denying the Vastness when you say, "My mind has to understand it."

So, a spiritual person is one who has racked his or her brain for many years, to try to achieve understanding. They have done every yoga conceivable, gone through Zen, all of it. And at the end, they realize: "I am who I am." Maybe their health has improved, maybe it hasn't. Some people follow vegetarian austerities and become ill, while other people follow them and become well. We can put no rules on the Vastness. Please understand what a foolish enterprise it is to try to place rules on the Vastness. It is like standing on the edge of the sea, holding up your hand and saying, "No more waves! I understand what makes these waves crash on this shore and I'm standing here to say, no more waves." It is impossible.

Whenever you become involved with a deep spiritual teaching, one of the things that goes through your mind as a disciple is the thought that the guru, the master, the roshi, knows something you don't know. And if only you can be good enough, meditate long enough, practice enough austerities, and surrender enough, the master will bring you the secret key to your unfoldment. Let us say this is true. The master knows and you do not; he has the key and you do not. Who then is in control of your Enlightenment, you or the master? And what if the master does not like you? What if the master does not like the color of the shirt you wear or what you do on Saturday nights? He can withhold this Enlightenment from you forever. Or, if he happens to be a judgmental sort of fellow, he can tell you that you are not ready now. He can tell you to come back in another lifetime, how about three lifetimes? Does that make you feel strong, powerful, and in control of your own Awareness? I think not. Or, let us say you feel it is not the master who has the 'secret,' it is you. *You* have the key, but oh my God, you don't know where it is. How are you going to find it? And then you go through the same process with yourself. If you are more austere, fast more, meditate more, or read more, then you will give *yourself* the key. Again you are in an impossible position. You are asking yourself to

61

tell yourself something that you are withholding from yourself. Does that make any sense at all? To me it does not.

I would like to suggest that we are talking about the wrong problem. The problem is not that you don't know, the problem is that you think there is something to find, that there is something other than this moment that you need. You keep thinking that there is something you are missing, something you lack. If you continue this 'linear' type of thinking, you will go on searching for the 'key' for lifetimes. Your ego will remember all those Saturday night parties, so you'll have to wait three years for your key since you are such a sinner. Always the ego is saying, "Don't worry, Realization is just around the corner, hang on, hang on! Some wonderful person will come and speak to you and you will be Enlightened." As long as you think someone else has to give it to you, you will not find Enlightenment, because that makes you a 'seeker.' As we have said before, you are either a 'seeker' or you are a 'finder.' And seekers keep seeking, and finders realize they cannot understand it; do not need to understand it, and can only live it.

And this is the only mystery that I would like to talk about. I say to you again and again, *this is it*. This experience of moment to moment living is it. Life is not going to get 'better,' my friends. Could you please understand that the greatest gift that you could give yourself is to accept the fact that it is not going to get any 'better.' *This* is the face of the Divine. If you keep waiting for a future time, you are just creating more and more tomorrows, more and more somedays. This day is every day. And this day is *all* days. *This day is it*! When you stop seeking and realize that you cannot force your brain anymore, cannot discipline your body anymore, that you have done all you can and tried as hard as you know how, and now you just feel helpless—the minute you say that and mean it, the ego surrenders. It is ego that has set up the game of seeking, and it is ego that 'dies' when you recognize that you can't win. The minute *that* knowledge moves into your consciousness, ego ceases to have power, ceases to motivate you, ceases to move you through the paces of your life. It just lays down and surrenders. In truth, ego never dies, it just surrenders.

The best game ego has is the spiritual game. This game is incredibly powerful because it makes you superior to everyone around you. Why? Because you are seeking God. And everyone knows that to seek God is the highest good. So you seek God, and you feel powerful, stronger and wiser, more and more holy, until finally you find the people around you can't stand you. You are so holy that your very presence makes them guilty. And it is because your ego is going on endlessly, making assessments and judgments. Remember, there are no rules for anyone. Enlightenment happens when it happens, when it happens. If the rules worked, many of you in this room would already be Enlightened. *If* the rules worked. But they don't. Rules are built on one man's or one woman's Enlightenment. And out of this vast amazing event, tomes are written about how it happened and what people should do to come to the same understanding. And the one who has had this experience knows that the truth cannot be spoken, but does the best they can in words. And the minute the words go out, down they go in writing and then for thousands of years, people read them and live by them. Some of you have been seeking Enlightenment for many lifetimes, again and yet again, and the depressing thing is, if you continue to have this idea that God is something other than you, doing whatever it is you are doing this moment, you will be at it many lifetimes more.

Please look at the people who try to be 'virtuous.' It is an incredibly difficult struggle, and their main hallmark is that they don't have any fun! For hundreds of years the idea has grown that if you're going to see God you must quit having fun. Because after all, you think that God doesn't know anything about fun. Yet it has been said that, "A sign of the presence of God is the presence of joy." That statement is more important than you think. Remember this please—when you move into a space within you that says you are doing fine, that you are moving along the Path, that things are under control and your life is rather calm, you can begin to feel righteous, to feel superior. That, to me, is the time to realize that something is very wrong. If you can make sense of your life, then you are using your mind. Life has no sense to it. Haven't you figured that out yet? Life is not this wonderful machine that goes into operation, and then relentlessly moves on for hundreds of years, following laws that you have made up! That isn't the way it goes. Again and again, you hear that God is spontaneous, creative, dynamic motion. If it is a machine that moves on relentlessly, following your laws, can you tell me where the spontaneity is? If you have that kind of mechanical idea in mind, then you are forgetting the basic substance of Life, which is joy, and it comes from the spontaneous movement of whatever is happening now. In that kind of movement comes Freedom. Then you can stop judging yourself. If you stop trying to become whatever it is you are trying to become and instead have the feeling that you are what you are, and *this* is the moment—your struggle stops. Some of you are afraid to have your struggle stop, because if it ends, how are you going to get Enlightened? Do you see the paradox in the mind? You must struggle toward Enlightenment, but you can only reach Enlightenment when your struggle stops.

The problem here is that you've addressed the wrong subject. You know, Ramana Maharshi says, "You are already Enlightened." And you say, "Yes, good, good," but you don't believe it. You put it on hold, telling yourself that some day you will think about it—but you don't believe it. Ramana says, "The only obstacle to your Enlightenment is the thought that you are not Enlightened." And you think, "Oh yes, good, good," but you don't believe it. But, either this man is a fool prattling lies, or he is speaking the truth. You decide. And if you decide that he is speaking truth, then would you please believe him when he says that the greatest and only obstacle to your Enlightenment is the thought that *you are not already Enlightened*! Believe him or not—but do not half-way believe him. It is the mind-ego-body that traps you in the middle.

How many of you are addicted to seeing yourself as a spiritual seeker? If you look carefully, you will find that view is the ego's greatest weapon for one-upmanship. A spiritual seeker is at the top of the pile, and everybody knows it! Many people play this game in order to feel better about themselves. Oftentimes people who have failed in other parts of their lives turn to the spiritual world thinking, "Well, I made a mess of the earth plane, but at least I can do something better on the other planes." Unfortunately, the earth plane and the other planes are one. You cannot jump over the earth plane and sit on heavenly clouds in a different state of consciousness. The easiest way to vaster states of understanding is the total, utter *acceptance* of this plane *exactly* as it is, and you *exactly as you are*, and your neighbors *exactly as they are*; and to love your neighbor as yourself! You cannot love your neighbor if you feel superior to him. This is called condescension, not Love!

How do you Love? You simply do the best that you can, with whatever and whoever is before you. Do, say, and feel what you are. Be *yourself* this day. And if you would stop trying so hard, my friends, you would quit being so hard on yourself, and then you would quit being so hard on others. Please understand, one who finds that the world is beneath them, who finds people negative, judgmental, evil, or undisciplined, is the kind of a person who has found themselves lacking; and in order to feel all right about themselves, projects out a world that is less than they are. This goes on endlessly, and it is not the answer.

If you think that this world was created out of a substance that was non-Divine, then you and I have nothing to say to each other. But if you believe that this world was created, and is still being created and sustained by what you call 'Divine Power,' then you must take the next step—if this is God's work, then let's do it! Are there two, God and the devil? Do you think separation is what is really going on? Do you know how those old ideas got started? It was very simple: a group of humans got together and said, "This spontaneous living is all right, but it is not very predictable, and we

65

ought to have a little more predictability. So let's make some rules. If we make some rules, then *we* will know how things will be." And you like predictability because then people don't give you any trouble. Unpredictable people are a pain, because they keep changing and you can't count on them. So you tell them they are not dependable, or not reliable, or not responsible. They are *inconvenient* because they change. And if *they* change you will have to change, and you may not like that. So you resist change, and call on all those great 'cosmic laws' that you have created to keep people in line. You have to be responsible, you have to be reliable, you have to be loving, and on down the list you have created. Do you realize how regimented your lives are? You have to decide what to eat and what not to eat, when to breathe and how to breathe, what to think and what not to think! How are you going to do that, my friends? How are you going to think what to think and what not to think? You have set out a tremendous job for yourself. And it is all humbug! You keep forgetting the basic premise: it is *all* Divine. If it is Divine, *then where is your preference?*

But you don't believe it is all Divine. The institution called church has taught you that there is such a thing as 'evil,' and evil is something to fight against, day and night, relentlessly. I do not see evil and I do not believe in evil. I believe there is *fear* and it is fear that makes people act in ways that are not loving to other people. There is no one born that does not have Love in them. No one. But fear clouds Love and says don't be Loving—for if you are Loving, you will be vulnerable; and if you are vulnerable, somebody will hurt you. If you can only accept that hurting is just hurting and that's that, and not spend all of your lives trying to get away from pain, you are going to find that your world changes entirely. Let it hurt you. Are any of you dead? All of you have been hurt, endlessly hurt, and you are still here, still alive and doing well. What has it done to you, this terrible thing? The *fear* of the pain you are running from is a phantom. You cannot have joy without the sorrow, they are two sides of the same world. So let people say 'bad' things about you, or to you. Does it really matter?

Let me tell you, my friends, the moment you hear the 'bad' words, you have a choice. You can drop your reaction to it, or you can play out the drama boldly, enjoying every moment of it. It doesn't matter! If you like to feel depressed, dejected, and guilty—fine, go ahead and do it. Do it boldly, with verve, vigor, and vitality! Be real about it. The difficulty comes when you say that you have no choice in all of this. *The thought that you are choiceless is what makes you vulnerable*. If you could once see that you are totally filled with choice, every instant, things would change. It is not the events that undermine you, *it is your response to them*. You have all heard this until you are tired. But if you really hear it once with all of your being, you will understand it is not the events that hurt you, it is your response to them.

What does self-illumination mean to you? Is it a feeling of oneness with everything around you? A feeling of joy, compassion, and life? I would ask you to look at what it is that is keeping those things from you now. If you look carefully, you will see it is your thoughts, relentlessly dwelling on fear from the past, fear of future loneliness, illness, guilt, whatever. You are caught, and you move between the two poles of past and future. Everyone says the way out is to quiet the mind. So you go through all the austerities to quiet the mind. But you don't have to go through austerities. You have to quiet your mind. And that is *all* you have to do! The best way to quiet it is *to be in the moment*. Your mind cannot be agitated if you are in *this* moment. If you are alive to this moment, alive to all that is within it; if you are here boldly, you are not thinking about the future, or ruminating over the past. You are so dynamically here, that heaven help us, you start to feel good! And that can be terrible. Do you know what an ethic you have in your culture about not feeling good? A child starts to feel good about himself, and the mother tells him not to be arrogant. If he or she says they are good at something they are reprimanded. Early on, you learn that to say that you are good at something is not acceptable. You know, a child that's beautiful may well make a statement about being beautiful, but people think she is conceited. *She* can observe her beauty, but she learns not to state that strength to herself, and more important, not to state it to other people. So where are you ever going to get your feeling of strength? You are not allowed to experience it, and the world is not going to give it to you because they don't want you to feel you are better than they are. Where can you get your sense of self, if the world cannot give it to you, and you cannot give it to yourself? When you accept yourself, your life, your world, and everyone and everything in it, all of a sudden, the energy that you have been using for years to *make* yourself acceptable is released.

You have beaten yourselves against the walls of your lives long enough, my friends. When you finally stop trying to be perfect, things will happen. You will begin to experience the peace and clarity you have been looking for. We keep telling you that you are all right the way you are, but I don't think many of you believe it. If it is the Divine that creates all, then the Divine has created and maintains your life, and it is all right, *exactly as it is.*

You are all weaving an incredibly vast and beautiful tapestry of moving Light, lifetime after lifetime, millions of you. From your limited consciousness, it is not possible for you to view that tapestry; but there will come a time in each of your understandings when you will find enough detachment to be able to see what you have created, all of you together, and will find it good. *You will!* This vast tapestry is what your life is all about. Many of you have had experiences where you have been able to see the threads of energy moving between and around you, and you *know* that there are undulating paths of Light that sustain and nourish you, and it is beautiful, alive, dynamic, deep, full, and totally wonderful. Because you are so close, and so busy weaving your own strand, you cannot see the boldness or the wonder of the whole. But when you do see it, you will not want to change one line, one incident, one moment; you will see that it is all absolutely perfect, exactly as it is, and you would feel the joy and the wonder of being a part of that. You are all part of that immensity, and it is beautiful! Try to see it that way, please.

Q: My ego will not allow me to look back on my life and see that in all those years I have learned nothing to make me wiser, more capable, or more spiritual.

If you look deeply enough, I think all of you will find yourself in the same position. You have lived long years out of an old idea of having to pull yourself up by your bootstraps, make your own way, be self-reliant, take care of yourself. All of these concepts have been built-in for lifetimes. If you will live in the moment, not budging one inch into past or future, you *will see* your relationship to the world. Pain comes, you experience it, pain goes. Emotion and thought come, you react and it goes. Your observation of it all will begin to build a different power around you. There will come increasing moments, then hours, then days, when those old thought forms will not manifest. You will find that you don't have to struggle so hard, that you don't have to be impressive, that you don't have to be wise—all of those old things begin to lose their grip on you. You will find yourself more happy, more joyful, in the moment of Life as it is unfolding. And the only way is to *do it*! You cannot 'unthink' things; all you can do is stay so powerfully aware in the moment that a new force begins to impress itself upon you—just as that old force has been impressed upon you. It will not take lifetimes to unbuild these things. When you begin to stay in the moment, what will come out of that, with no effort on your part, is another view, another sense of life. And the more you do this, the less grasp the past will have on you. It is only when the new takes over that the old drops away.

When you stay in the moment, and feel the power of who you are, you will see that you have made a misidentification. You have identified yourself with a small body/mind moving through time/space. All of your old rules apply to that body/mind. But that is not who you are! That is only a small fragment of the totality of who you are; and in the power of the moment comes the dawning of true vision. And then all of those rules, needs, and desires take a very pale second place to the Power of *who you really are*!. If this information is going to mean anything to anyone, it has to go beyond concepts and ideas, and move into practice. And the only practice that I really recommend is to stay in the moment. *This is it.* And it is beautiful!

In the moment, you will be so much more alive to all experiences, to all sights and sounds. When you are totally *here*, it is all so bold. You become bored with life because you think you know everything—but *you don't know anything*! And the reason you don't know anything is because every moment is new—and how could you know something that is always new? Life becomes exciting if you make each moment something new to experience. This newness is where the joy of Life comes from. Life is never old or finished; it is just as new and as young as the moment you were born.

TO BE A MASTER
27 March 1983
Albuquerque, New Mexico

This is the time of the Easter celebration, and in connection with that I would like to talk about Masters. A real 'man of God' is a Master. Jesus was called Master; the Buddha was called Master, as were many great teachers.

'Master' is an interesting word for it reflects a requirement that is an absolute necessity. To be a Master you must first be a master of your own life. You know at a deep level that you are a part of the on-going Divine process, but at the same time, you also know that there are areas of your psyche that you have not looked at. These are reflected in your conscious world as areas of fear. The reason that you fear those areas is that in not looking at them, you have not become master of that energy. To become a Master does not mean that you become skilled, but that you become *aware*.

Let us say that you have fear in the area of personal relationships. You are afraid to go into a relationship for fear of losing it, for if you lose it you will feel isolated, lonely and devastated. This is the fear that arises in your awareness. This is where you make the statement, "I feel fear, and so I know that I am not master here." And then your next step is to become master of that which you fear. Unfortunately, that is not what you usually do. Usually you settle for the status quo, a nice smooth surface of the 'lake,' so that you will not drown. And if that solution does not work, you try another. But each time you go on to another solution, you acquire a new level of fear because you have 'failed' so often. The pattern of failure is established.

What then is the way out? The real seeker becomes determined to find out *why* he is afraid. There is no one who does not have access to their own akashic record. So with a little contemplation, you can bring to your conscious awareness the major events in this and other lives that have caused you the conflict and the fear. This is not written in a book held by someone else to whom you must go for the information. It is always around you, but your conscious mind rejects the information as being only your imagination. Self-doubt comes in, and you accept it. A real Master says *no* to self-doubt because he has the deep desire to see his fears and free himself from them. He will use any tool available. So with introspection, you will get pictures and feelings around your fear, and you will become more and more aware of the facets of that fear. Total feeling tones will be presented clearly to you, and you will know without question what the face of your fear looks like. Once you know that, you are in a position to become fear-less.

Here is one way I would suggest that you work with your fears. When you sit there, and the fear is upon you, the first and foremost question to ask is what does it *feel* like? Your fear has a *feeling* to it, a tone to it. It grabs you at some point within your body, and it is very strongly present. The mind then takes hold of that feeling, starts to talk about it, and tries to escape from it. But you never just *sit with it*. When you do sit with the feeling, right then you will discover that the fear is not all-encompassing. It is present, and you will know it, but at the same time you will also know that there is a lot of you that is not involved in the fear. Once you know this as an experiential part of your reality, you will gain the courage to stay with that fear until you understand it. If you think you *are* fear, if you think there is nothing in your being except terror, then you must run from it, for life is intolerable in the face of that terror. When you understand from your experience that there is also present a vast amount of power, balance, stability, compassion, and even good humor, then it is different.

It is as though you had injured your finger, but the rest of your body is all right. You do not take such extreme measures as jumping from a cliff because your finger hurts. You draw into you courage and confidence, because the rest of you is in fine shape. It is your lack of understanding of the situation, of the fact that your fear is only one small part of you, that makes you so vulnerable. Once you know from your own experience and awareness that you are so much more than your fear, the rest of the 'wiseness' which surrounds you can begin to operate. When you are in terror you do not think clearly. All you think of is escape. The problem is that the fear does not know how to escape. The Master does. So if you will call on the rest of your being to address this one partial problem, then in the quietude of just staying with it, you will come to an awareness of what to do about it. You do not believe this because you have not tried it. This is a way of life. Mastery is a way of life! You cannot be a Master one hour a week. You have to be a Master on an ongoing basis, which means that every time you feel a fear, no matter how small (and it is better to begin with the small ones) you address it. Any fear that comes up is like the tip of an iceberg— there is much more under the surface not available to you. When you begin to address even the small ones you will get in touch with what fear really is to you. For each of you it is a little different. Do not allow any of the pieces of fear to move away and escape your scrutiny. In so doing, you will move into Mastery. The more that you call on the Wisdom around you for an answer, the better things will go.

Many of you put yourselves willingly and willfully into stress positions. That is the wisest thing you can do if you want to become a Master. It is possible that those of you who have very safe and comfortable lives are in that state because you have not allowed yourselves to courageously follow those inner promptings that would lead you into areas of difficulty. Perhaps the reason your life is sweet and smooth is not because you are totally Enlightened, but because you have the chessmen all set up on the board to your satisfaction and nothing is awry. But you will either have to move the pieces, or your deep Self will move them for you. You can only hold your life at status quo for so long. Your deep Self knows what is needed in order for you to get on with the job of dealing with your unfinished patterns and your job is not to pat yourself on the head for the wonderful life you are having. Under those circumstances, the deep Self is just as likely to cause a great wind to blow across your chessboard, and the pieces will start to sway and fall. Congratulations, now you do have a problem!

You do not have to wait for your chessmen to be blown away to see where your next move should be. You know it. It might be in relationship; it might be in your job. It could be any number of things—and you know what it is. Because you are afraid, and it is so comfortable to sit in your chair and watch the television, you don't take the next step. But it is the next step that keeps you moving through your life. You are not meant to live your lives like robots, just being happy. The whole purpose of this life is to keep moving, to keep going deeper and yet deeper into your Self. A Master is one who has gone into all parts of his psyche, has found it all, and turned away from nothing. All that is presented is accepted, no matter how seemingly dark or dismal. It is *all* embraced.

Perhaps you are someone who knows without question that their life is not in alignment, and yet refuses to admit that their relationships are probably dull and boring—and that people around them are probably dull and bored! Your life has become stagnant. If you drag yourself awake every day with the feeling that it's just another day to be 'gotten through,' then please realize that you are stuck. You can be stuck at age five, or eighty-five, or anywhere in between. The movement of life does not stop until you leave your body. It continues to the end, and any time you find that lack of feeling, you are stuck. I am not saying that you should give up your houses or your apartments, and rush off to a new place in your necessity to make changes. But I do feel that you should ask yourselves where you are refraining from movement out of fear. Where have you stopped for fear that if you move on, your life will become more difficult? You will find that place if you look and when you do you will not be able to let that fear go. So don't look unless you are ready to deal with it. Once you have brought it to your awareness, you will not get away, for you cannot 'double-play' the game. You cannot fool both your conscious and your unconscious self. So you will begin to move, in one way or another.

I do not mind it when you have problems because I understand that it is through those so-called problems that you make your movement into Mastery. There are areas of fear that must be uncovered, and you uncover them not by running away, but by confronting them courageously. Mastery comes from understanding where your fear originates. The minute you understand *why* you are afraid, you can begin to unravel the strands that have kept you in fearful bondage. And some of those strands may reach beyond this lifetime.

Let us say that you fear financial difficulty but see no reflection of that in your life. You are not on the verge of starvation, but you still fear poverty. If that is a powerful fear and feels inappropriate at the present time, it might not have originated in this lifetime—but then neither did you! If you could take a deep breath and broaden your view of yourself, and see that you are the present but ongoing product of an endless number of experiences from many lifetimes, you would give yourself more space for understanding. Question where and what your real fear is all about. Again, bring pictures and feeling tones to your consciousness from other times and places. Even the most rational of you will have to incorporate into your understanding the difference between yourself as a young boy dying of starvation by the side of a road in India, for example, and your position today. Once you understand from whence the fear comes, you become wise about your own process. You will not be free of your fears until you bring them into consciousness. The way to alleviate financial fears is not to have many jobs but to track that fear to its source and understand the relationship between your past fear and your present life.

Ill health and the fears arising from that situation rarely originate in this lifetime. If you have dealt with the fear of illness in the past, clarity will be there about present illnesses. The problem is that the memory or feeling tone from many past illnesses floods into the present. You have forgotten that when you face a present illness, you are *all right*! Any illness is appropriate to the time and situation, and fits perfectly into the mosaic of your life. You fail to see that your life, as you are living it, is just fine. No matter what the extremity, it has deep, ultimate, and beautiful meaning. You are trapped by a fear which does not arise from the present situation and the 'bleed-through' is such that you cannot isolate it out. You do not fear what is now, but an old fear that overtakes you.

The same thing can happen with relationship. It is time for two people to move in different directions, but one may have unfaced hidden fears from past-life experiences and tries to hang on to the other. He or she may feel the terrible desolation of loss from past relationships that will keep them from understanding the rightness of the separation. To bring these things into consciousness is the only way to save yourself. Every time you feel fear, look carefully to see if it comes from the present situation or a 'bleed-through' of the past or a combination of both. In any difficulty, you must be totally present in the moment to call on the Power that surrounds you to give you the clarity that you need. What did the Christ mean when he said, "Come unto me, all who are heavy laden, and I will refresh you"? It means that within the auric field of every entity that has ever walked the earth plane, there is a vast Wisdom and Understanding of the rightness of your life as it is expressing itself in this moment. That feeling of 'rightness' is what gives you the release from your burden of fear. It is expressed as Christ-consciousness, Buddha Mind, Divine Understanding, or whatever else you choose to call it. It is that part of you that knows the perfection of what you are, exactly as you are *now*, without any changes at all. When you refuse to run from fear, when you decide to stay with and understand the perfection of who you are, the vaster vision will come to you—clearly, powerfully, and purposefully. You do not have to be 'Enlightened.' Jesus never said, "Only those of you who are Enlightened may come to me and I will refresh you!" He went instead to the most down-trodden, to the most lacking in understanding, and he called them. There wasn't a Ph.D. in the crowd. He knew that fear was a very large factor in their being.

If you look only at your fear, you will not see the rest of your vast Being. The minute you ask for vision, for release, for understanding, for peace of heart in the midst of difficulties; when you no longer ask that they be removed by some Big Daddy, but stay with them because they are there, you will realize that your present difficulty is only a small part of you, and the rest is doing very well, thank you. Out of the wisdom and the depth of the rest of you, you will come into conscious acceptance of whatever the pain is, whatever the fear is, whatever the situation is. And from that perception you can accept and embrace it and perhaps even enjoy it.

You do not allow yourself to enjoy anything that even resembles pain, suffering, or fear. By trying to keep those away from you, you cut off part of your life force. I am asking you to commit to becoming a Master of yourself. Until you accept and integrate your fear areas into your life, you will live a life that is only half alive. In the midst of *any* extremity, however painful, however dangerous, there is always the amazing power of Life—and you cannot live Life fully if you are afraid. If you are afraid, how can you be spontaneous? How can you open your heart? You are afraid to open your heart for fear that the darkness will flood in and overwhelm you and isolate you. Many of you have had the courage to move into new situations or new lifestyles, and if you stay awake every day, you will soon know why. You move through life not knowing why you are doing what you do. Keep your awareness on yourself in the moment, day after day, and you will know what is happening.

If you feel fear in a new situation, just stop a moment and ask what you are afraid of. What is it about the situation that has triggered your fear and has it arisen from beyond the context of that moment? Ask yourself *what it is that you need that you are not getting*? When you are afraid, it is because you want something and you are not getting it. You are inclined to think of needs in terms of the physical, such as needing more people, more love, or more money. But basically, what you are saying is that you want something to make you feel fearless. So, what will make you feel fearless in this situation?

For example, you go to a job interview and the person is very brusque. You may begin to feel fear. What is it you are afraid of? Are you afraid you will be rejected, that you will be found unworthy or not good enough? Once you understand what part of your fear is from past rejection, the present feeling will be lessened. Does it really matter all that much whether you get that particular job? Does it really matter whether that one person sees you as worthy? Should you feel sorry for yourself because someone has said that he would rather hire someone else? When you understand what it is you are looking for that you didn't receive (approval?), you will be able to let go of that particular situation. Even if you were to apply for a job that you had no real training for, you would still feel rejection if you were not hired. There is something about the human psyche that feels the need for approval from everyone his universe. Let's remove some of the strain by suggesting that you split your need for approval 50/50. So that 50% of the time you will have approval, and 50% of the time you will not. This could be a great relief! You might even be happy when you had made your 50% for the day. No one who is being himself is going to be approved of all of the time.

If those with the power and the wisdom of the Christ could capture the hearts of so few, why do you think that you should be able to do better? It is not possible, and it is not necessary. Your life does not need to have total acceptance to be totally beautiful. There is only one place where you need acceptance to make your life beautiful—and that is *acceptance of yourself, exactly as you are*! That will come from courageous self-observation. From that intro-

80

spection you will learn that you are absolutely fine just the way you are. There is an amazing wonder about Life expressing itself through you, exactly as you are, *now*. It does not come from asking people on your block if they love you; it comes from an inner acceptance of all the things you need to know about yourself. That is the pivot point of your life. The whole world could love you, but if you do not love yourself, you would not even notice. The opposite is also true—the whole world could disapprove of you, but if you love yourself, you would not even notice. Accept yourself within you and the entire world becomes totally acceptable.

Q: During a recent illness I had much fear, but by centering on the Infinite Creator it all dissolved. Am I an escapist?

If that process works for you, I suggest that you continue to do it. That is not escapism; that is knowing where to go. Many times in extremity, there is such a thing as 'grace'. But most of you, most of the time, cannot sit around waiting for it. *You* have to be the source of your own 'grace.' The Source is infinitely compassionate, and energies do move in at times to uplift and transform. But if you are waiting for that on a day-by-day basis and it does not happen, you are stuck. The Master says, "I am going to do what I can to deal with this fear." When you sit with it and *feel* it, you make it a sister or brother to you, and the wholeness of the fearful experience moves in and begins to teach you. When you run, you never learn what you are afraid of, you only feel the effects of your fear. Stay steady, firm, courageous and you will become *exhilarated*. You become exhilarated when you decide that you *will be* the master in your own house. It comes from that Vast part of your being that begins to empower you. You have the right to call on all of the power of your Being to help you through any extremity. But if you do not call on it, it will not move. Your finite ego-self has will and when you call, the power will be there. Peace of heart is your right no matter what your life might look like and in the midst of any extremity. Claim it! Who will be master in your house—fear or you? Your choice. No event comes to you without absolute meaning, depth, and purpose. Isolate the fear into your 'finger' and call on the whole 'body' to clarify it. Do not fall into the habit of asking other people to clarify your fears. They can point the way, but they can't know because they are not you. *You* have to be the Master. Once you decide to be Master, life takes on a very different meaning. Then no extremity is unwelcome, no adversity comes without a mitigating grace. Everything you do and experience becomes a part of the process to deepen your understand,ing of self. This is what the job is about, my friends—understanding the Self.

Can one create prosperity by turning fear around and visualizing prosperity?

That would not be my suggestion for some of you don't need prosperity. My basic premise is that your own deep Self knows precisely what you need, not to keep you happy, but to evolve your inner Self. Some people evolve much better in poverty. They will move when in extremity, but do nothing when things are pleasant. Understand the problems that are there and use them for your spiritual unfoldment. If you want prosperity, then go for that. But if your deep Self knows that you will learn more from poverty, then you will again be in poverty. You are always presented with what is needed for your growth. You have had many lifetimes with great prosperity. In this life of duality you have to experience it all— poverty and wealth, illness and health, murder and being murdered, the whole spectrum is needed. There is nothing wrong with being poor, except in feeling poor. You are here to see your fears, and if poverty brings up fear in you, that's wonderful. If there is no longer need for that fear, you will, without doing anything to bring it about, experience wealth, or sufficiency. Wealth is not for most of you. Materialism and money are great difficulties to overcome on the earth plane, for they give you too many choices, too many buffers to make your life look sweet, so that you forget you are miserable. If you have learned the deep soul lesson about the fear around poverty and have completed the cycle, without you doing one thing, prosperity will move in.

Will not focusing on health overcome fear of illness?

You can pretend to focus on health by saying that you 'believe in health,' but until you get to the root of why you fear ill health, you will only be able to see illness. Being ill is not so bad. Being poor is not so bad. Being *anything that is manifesting* is not so bad! You will have to take your turn at experiencing all of it. If you want to work at manifesting wealth, or health, that is wonderful. It can happen, especially if you work at it very hard. But I am asking you to understand why the inner Self manifests illness for you. Because there is a deep fear within you that needs to be seen and released; and when you release it it is finished for all time. Then in the next lifetime you will not have to *try* to be healthy, you will be healthy. You will be ready to deal, moment to moment, with whatever is manifesting. Any time you uproot your fear it is finished, not only for this lifetime, but for all of them. Each of you is manifesting what it is that you need to be learning. You are not all ill; you do not all need to learn the same lesson. You have finished many lessons, but the lessons that remain will not be completed until their root causes are removed. Focusing on the *fear* of illness is the thing that will bring you to health.

THE TWELVE STRANDS OF POWER
22 January 1984
Albuquerque, New Mexico

We have often spoken of the fact that you are on a journey. In your everyday life, you would not make a trip to the mountains without the proper equipment, but you have forgotten that when you set out on this life journey, you came prepared. And so I would like to remind you of some of your equipment.

Science is becoming more aware of the fact that you are energy in motion, sometimes fast, sometimes slow and that motion embodies in it various colors in lighter and darker bands. Part of your basic earth plane 'equipment' includes *twelve strands of power*. These twelve energy strands are also a part of your awareness and can be readily identified by you if you will take the trouble to look for them. The difficulty is that you are accustomed to viewing these strands as 'problems,' rather than as 'strands of power.' One of the things you came to accomplish when you took form on this planet was to recognize that these twelve strands have been split, each into two parts. Your job is to merge them together again and bring them back into balance and harmony. You experience difficulties in your life when one or more of these strands moves through you in an unbalanced state. When the job of balancing them is finished, you will move on to areas of consciousness where there are other powers not available to you on the earth plane.

When you move into an incarnative pattern and begin to bring the twelve strands into balance, you will experience feelings of love without personality, wisdom without superiority, power without arrogance, and aliveness without specialty. All of this results in that wonderful state of Awareness which you call 'bliss.' The body resonates with a knowingness of its own wonder, but the wonder is not personal, for you understand that it moves through all creation. So, in your life you must come to acknowledge the power that moves through you, identify which strand is out of harmony, and then balance it. This is not hard to do, if you are clear about those three things. Real balancing brings a feeling which many of you have known—that *all of life is as it should be*. This does not mean that you will never have conflicts, it means that it does not matter what difficulties you might have. As you may observe, there are those of you who are in states of great physical difficulty whose being still resonates with acceptance, wonder, love—and even joy! Do not look to your external situations, but to your inner feelings, to find your areas of imbalance.

Many descriptions of the twelve strands have been brought to your awareness over the years. They can be found buried in your spiritual literature and enshrined in old myths and legends. They can point the way, but the balancing of the strands are not beyond your own wisdom.

Let us speak about some of the main strands. We will start with the strand you would call *aloneness*. You have, in your present culture, lost the power inherent in the wisdom of being alone, for you have confused this state with loneliness. When this strand is in harmony, you will know that you contain all that you need *within* yourself and you do not really *need* anyone else. This does not mean that you cannot enjoy, fully participate with, and admire others, but you will know that you have created the balance within your own being and you can stand powerfully and blissfully alone. You make your lives very difficult when you ignore this strand. This has become the age of 'togetherness.' You are together all the time and even if no one else is around, you almost always have that universal mandala, the television, to take the place of people. What you need to experience is the bliss that comes from being alone with yourself. If you ignore the wonder and the power of this strand, you will stay in a state of needy imbalance in your world, always looking to others outside yourself to make you feel all right. Even those of you who have been so wise as to construct your lives so that you are alone are in a state of ambivalence about it. And this very ambivalance is what impedes your learning. Instead of stating that you are alone because it is only by being *with yourself* that you can learn *about yourself*, you go around feeling lonely and left out. Continuing relationships that are no longer meaningful because you are afraid of being alone creates the fear that brings about the imbalance that can keep you 'stuck' on this strand for lifetimes.

If you wish to learn about your unbalanced strands, look to the fantasies which come to you and fill you with anxiety. Look to the things that you fear. The phantoms are in your psyche, and they represent your imbalances. For example, you might have anxiety about money. Some of you worry if you don't have money, and some of you worry if you do! Money is just today's symbol for security.

What is the strand behind money? The ability to *trust* life is the strand that stands behind these anxieties. You have a deep feeling that 'people are not to be trusted'; that they do not have your best interests at heart. I would suggest a alternative view. You are all an on-going flood of entities, moving, extending, creating, and becoming Aware. And you are doing *the best you can* at this moment! You do not move in random patterns. If you would acknowledge that *you* are not moving at random, then you would see that others also are not. If another entity moves out of a pattern of intimacy with you and into another, be aware that this is not a haphazard movement. You are afraid that your life might become difficult when these patterns are broken. And so to feel safe, you try putting the pieces back into a familiar pattern by pulling that person or a different person into your life. I am not asking you to trust that others will remain in your life forever or that you will never experience pain. I am asking that you trust that your universe is moving *precisely* in accordance with your own deepest needs and whatever is here is present in power, and what is present is needed. If the pattern never changed, you would become very bored. You

87

are here for the power of the ride, and not for the sameness of the scenery. Please, learn to enjoy the changing scenery! So many of you try to cling to the past to prevent changes in your lives. You talk in the present about events long over to avoid the new and 'frightening' changes you are afraid might come. These fears are only in your mind. Your deep Self will move you to where you need to go for the maximum experiences of your lifetime. I would ask you to trust that this is so, and that this strand has the power to make your life ever new and exciting.

How can you approach any strand with power, rather than with weakness? The answer is by having another view of yourself. Originating with the Source from which all of these strands arise and moving out in multi-colored rays, you were created. You have chosen to slow down the Divine energy, so that you appear as form, as a body. As you move through life, whether in negative or positive movement, you are feeling life. When you feel that life, you are feeling the movement of the 'strands.' That *awareness of movement* is the power you need to approach any strand with strength. When 'death' of the body comes, the strands move on and you say, "the spirit has left the body." If you wish to approach the balancing of these strands with mastery, be aware of any kind of movement within your body and ask yourself what strand is out of balance. Resistance to positive or negative movement is a sign that you have come upon one of your unbalanced strands. After you have identified the unbalanced strand, ask yourself what it is that needs to be done. Do not act as though you don't know, because in fact, you do know a tremendous amount. Ask what needs to be done, *now!* Not at a more convenient time, but at the moment when you are feeling the pressure of the imbalance. Be aware of your refusal to accept given situations and solutions. Do not try to protect, defend, or rationalize. Just ask, and the answer will come. It will come as a knowingness or insight or feeling. It may be as simple as 'just let go,' or 'don't make it so important.' There are any number of messages and solutions that you will give yourself, but you will get no answers unless you address the question. With the problem there always arises the solution; for they are both energy and they come together. Then you must have the courage to act upon what you have told yourself.

The reason you find all of this difficult is because you have given up your mastery. You have given it to other people, who can help you in part, I agree, but who are not in a position of knowing what is best for you. Because their strands are not in the same degree of balance/imbalance as yours and they have not had the same life experiences, they cannot really answer your questions for you. You live in the century of authority, the authority of other people. You have lost your own power, and so when the time comes that you need it, you don't believe you have it! Please recognize one thing; you did not come into this life without the equipment necessary for the journey. *You do not have to live your life off balance.* It is *your* reponsibility to discover what is best for you and bring peace and harmony into your life.

Another strand with which many of you have difficulty is the strand of *wisdom*. You do not have to be an intellectual genius to balance this strand, because the balancing of wisdom has nothing to do with information you have spent your life accumulating. Stored knowledge depends only on how much brain power you have decided to actualize in this lifetime. The balancing of this strand has to do with understanding that true wisdom is the ability to observe and accept everyone's point of view with equanimity. Real 'wisdom' is the inner knowingness that each individual is presenting his own truth from his own perspective. The wise one accepts this without challenge and feels no need to defend his own position or to destroy that of another. You do not feel threatened by others when your wisdom is in balance! Wisdom cannot be experienced through words or information found in any book, even in the greatest of them. *Wisdom has to be lived.* It is your own sense of what is totally appropriate for *you*, this moment. What is wise for you on Thursday may not be wise for you on Sunday because you are not the same. Wisdom unfolds itself deeply within you when you begin to be responsible for finding your own truth, and do not impose it on any other being. You are not being responsible when you feel that what is true for you then must be true for all and your job is to reveal that 'truth' to everyone else. People have a hard time deciding who is the 'wisest' and many relationships are built on this struggle for 'one-upmanship.' Wisdom is something to seek, and I highly recommend it, but I ask you not to measure its lack or abundance in other people's psyches. You do not need any outer agreement to validate your own wisdom. Trust your own inner feelings to show you your truth.

I would speak also of the strand which we will call *responsibility*. This is a concept that confuses many. You are told that you are responsible for your life *and* for all that happens in it. You are also told that you are responsible for not causing any inconvenience or discomfort to others and for moving with harmlessness through your world. This word responsibility and your concept of it can be frightening, because you are afraid that things you have done will end up hurting other people. It is a great burden to feel responsible for all of the ultimate chaos that might arise out of one of your decisions. You have a child, and you feel responsible for all that the child does, throughout his entire lifetime. The child gets into trouble and you feel it is your fault. You have a car accident which injures or kills someone and you feel guilty. You give information that does not turn out well and you feel responsible. It is endless.

That is not the kind of responsibility that I am talking about. I will tell you again that you do not move in random patterns. You move in a cohesive, beautiful, exciting, extending pattern of power. The responsibility of which I speak is the realization that, if you observe the movement of your life and do not like what you see, it is *you* that must make the changes in it. Growth comes through change; exciting growth through responsible change. You may observe that your life pattern has not been rewarding, but you hesitate to make changes because you are familiar with the old patterns and comfortable with their predictability, even though the patterns have not been satisfying. I would remind you, that you have, within your own being, the ability to make responsible choices; choices that will create a life pleasing to you. There are two sides to the strand of responsibility. One side presents a person who wanders aimlessly through life with no responsibility and the other presents a person who feels responsible for everything. Both are out of balance. How do you know when you need to make new choices? When you look at your life and see parts of it that are not rewarding to you or to others. Then, *you* have to be responsible for becoming aware of what new choices would restore that balance again. But that is not what usually happens. You usually try to find some justification for continuing your old pattern, blaming other people for the way it is. Growth comes when you begin to assess your life, see that there is a need for change, and go within yourself to make that change. *Any choice you have made, you can change.* Accepting the responsibility of making your own choices in your life will give you the power to move in your world with strength and confidence.

There is one other strand that we will mention; that of *power in the manifest world.* When faced with difficulty, some people tend to get depressed and discouraged, and some tend to feel falsely that nothing is ever wrong. This is the area of power or powerlessness as it manifests on the physical plane. When you are in a state of depression, balance can be achieved when you realize that depression comes from power you *possess*, but have not used. When you begin to feel depression, it is a signal to ask yourself what it is that is threatening you. You feel threatened because you are again afraid of change, and yet, depression can be an exciting signal that deep changes are about to be made. The changes that you are most comfortable with are the happy and pleasant ones. If you were to live a life where there was only pleasant change I think you would be bored. Your unpleasant changes move you more quickly to new areas in your life and it is the balancing of those strands of power that make life on the physical plane exciting.

The person who is addicted to seeing only the happy side of life and admits to no negative experiences is avoiding one of the things that they came for—to balance the negative and positive polarities. You cannot balance something that you cannot feel and if you refuse to feel your fears or your so called negative side, you cannot live life to its fullest. Those who insist that 'nothing is ever wrong' do so out of the unconscious fear that they would not be able to handle whatever it is they think might be 'wrong.' Balancing for them means a willingness to examine *all* feelings and in so doing, find that they possess deep reservoirs of courage and abilities that they have kept hidden from themselves. And with this discovery comes the power to move in the manifest world with grace and beauty. When you begin to feel something unpleasant happening to you, acknowledge it and ask yourself, "What am I feeling? What am I afraid of? What is being presented, and how can I work with it?" You have yourself programmed so that you are the first to know what is 'wrong' with you through the feelings recorded in your body. And through those feelings, you can recognize power, both when it is blocked and when it is moving. You have the game set up for maximum awareness, but you have to pay attention to what is going on. When you present yourself with any difficulty, your solution is always contained within the balance of the 'twelve strands.'

Q: Why have you specified 'twelve' strands?

You have been told that there are seven chakras. I agree, but you also have five more, and those five are the ones I have just been talking about. You refer to them as 'chakras' and I refer to them as 'strands.' The seven chakras or strands that are most easily observed in the body are in the spinal area, and you are most aware of them when power is moving through them. These seven chakras concern survival and sexuality, balance, emotion, heart, will, visionary perception, and a higher state of consciousness. That which you call a higher state of consciousness is only the beginning of the movement into the next higher twelve strands. In truth, you are an energy field which has twelve points of power. When you move into a state of harmony, it is because those strands are balanced. Once they are balanced and you leave the earth plane, more strands are then added to you. I can testify from my own experience that bliss can become even more blissful. Think of the increased power and joy you will feel when you have balanced another twelve strands. It is an ever-expansive, exciting extension, where you are given more and more power to balance. But you cannot leave the earth plane until you have the present twelve strands taken care of, for if these were not balanced and you were given an additional twelve, you can imagine the chaos. You would not be able to handle them and you would be a danger, not only to yourself but to other entities. So, to move from one state of awareness to another, you must have those powers in balance.

This game was not set up to be a 'mystery,' but for *mastery*. I would again ask you to pay close attention to your own areas of resistance and in the moment of feeling that resistance, address the issue. The wonder of being human is that you are not only the computer, but you are also the computer programmer. You have the ability to understand instantly what is going on within you. Please remember that you know what you need to know, when you need to know it. If you think you don't know, it means that you are not yet willing to listen. But the wonder of the human psyche is that you can never stay where you are.

The five additional chakras or 'strands of power' that we have been talking about are mobile. The power of responsibility, for example, activates and moves through the seven more stationary 'centers' as do the other powers. They are in a state of constant motion and do not fit into the 'straight line' pattern of the seven chakras. When these powers move, they can activate and interact with different parts of you at different times. The survival chakra and the strand of trust, for instance, will have their turn at balancing each other. Thus, the strands and centers present many combinations and opportunities for you to balance your energies.

I am often asked, in what way is this world an illusion? Part of what you have created on this earth, from a combination of the strands and your so-called ego, does not endure and what does not endure is 'illusory.' The agonies that you create for your children by being 'bad parents' do not endure; so seen from a level beyond the body form, they are truly illusory. The difference between illusion and Reality is that Reality *never ceases to exist*; illusion rises, has form, and disappears. You are all made up of one substance, so when you perceive more than one, illusion is present. When a set of strands has been balanced, it is done and you do not have to do the same job over again in other lifetimes. The strands are eternal, do not come from this earth, and have nothing to do with form. They arise from the Source and are always with you. At the same time, they are useful in joining with form. You enliven form and you ignite it. The form dies, but the power of the strand does not. Aren't you glad that the illusory thoughts and feelings that you now have will not endure forever. Yesterday has already gone, as has a part of your own pattern. It was born and enlivened by your power, and then it died. Your power remains. The form has disappeared.

The doctrine of eternal punishment is perhaps the most crippling doctrine on the earth plane. It is the greatest travesty against the Createdness that I know of. It simply *is not true* but it has put tremendous fear into your psyche. No matter what you have created, once the power is removed, the form passes away and you are not responsible unto the 'third generation,' or for all time. Do the best you can to balance your strands and grant everyone else the same privilege. Trust that you and they are not moving at random. Your children chose you as parents because your struggle to balance your particular set of strands was exactly the challenge they needed. You always select the challenge you need.

This is not a random universe. Freedom comes from the knowledge that whatever illusions you have created will die. The wonder of the strands is what you call *eternity*. The balance is what you take with you to the 'next world' and out of that balance comes the new life, with new opportunities for growing and sharing. Illusions die; only the Real remains.

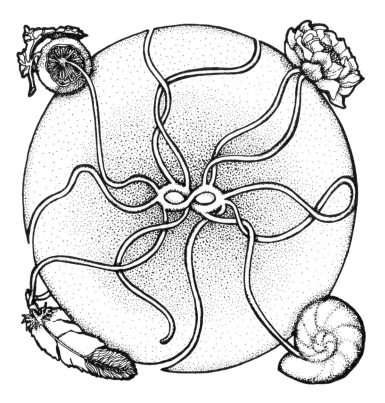

ADVANCED ENERGY FIELDS
13 January 1985
Albuquerque, New Mexico

Let us begin with an obvious statement: emergencies are not restricted to the earth. As above, so below and the high and the low reflect each other. With that in mind, but without any kind of agitation around it, I would like to move into an area that has not been relevant until now.

Many times I have shared with you the necessity of paying attention to your lives, but I come now with another statement that I ask you to take seriously. We have told you that there has been a tremendous increase in the amount of energy that is being sent to the earth plane for your absorption, transmutation, and increased awareness. You call it the New Age. We call it *advanced energy fields*. The difficulty with advanced energy fields is that you do not know what they contain, because if you did, they would not be advanced. They would be similar to those you now experience. Advanced energy fields call upon humanity to do things differently than humanity has been doing in past years, perhaps in the past few thousand years. This means that each of you, in your own way, is going to have to begin to build new inroads for this energy. Many of you are now experiencing tremendous energy overloads. You become confused or bewildered, and you may not understand why. There is nothing in your life that is particularly disruptive, but some things in the normalcy of a life which was normal for so long is changing. Relationships, jobs, even movement in the world is becoming more difficult.

You have put out the call for higher consciousness, for expansion. You want to break the boundaries and be alive with newness, power, and excitement. We have listened and are responding by

97

sending these advanced energy fields to you. You do not, at this moment, have in your bodies the means to incorporate that energy without being physically shaken up. Many long time meditators are finding that they cannot sit quietly anymore. When they sit, everything begins to buzz, they feel nervous and uneasy. Those of you who do sweat lodge sometimes feel that something is missing. I see people trying to take care of this uneasiness through physical means: put more rocks on the fire and make them hotter, or sit longer in meditation and maybe you will be still. People who pray are praying harder; yet none of this does it.

What then is required of you? Building new inroads in a physical body, so that you can incorporate higher frequencies, ends up being a personal matter. You are wondrous power centers, filled with trigger points of alive awareness. You are dead to most of these. Usually that is not a problem, but when this new energy comes in, it hits those points and jolts the physical. All over the world, people are responding to the increased energy in their own way and for the most part, they do not know what to do with it. This new power is going to change a great many things, from the weather to your own response to everyday life. And this is what I would like to focus on today.

My friends, you must find a way to take care of the increased energy, or you're going to find yourself in very volatile situations around people and things that you truly care about; relationships, jobs, family. The energy is going to get stronger and you cannot be careless with it any more. *You cannot be careless any more.* That does not mean that I am asking for a group of people who think they have no problems, that their lives are beautiful even when they are falling apart. I am not asking you to fool yourselves or to fool each other. I am asking you to consider one thing: that you have within your psyche the capacity for *self-examination*, and that faculty must come forward at this time. Without self-examination, you will not be able to find creative, dynamic ways to move in your world as the power continues to increase. You will run up against the walls of other people's impacted energy.

You must begin to believe that every difficulty that comes into your awareness is *your mirror*. *You* have called into your lives all these people and events to show you the parts of your consciousness that you have not yet wished to see clearly. This does not mean that if you have met a lecher, that you are one. It means that you have *judgment* against lechery. And be assured, if you judge against others, somewhere in your psyche, you have judged against yourself. And *that* is the place that you must go to and examine; that part of you that needs to feel superior and does so by judging another. Every time you judge, my friends, understand what you are doing. You are stepping on somebody's neck in order to stand up that much higher, not in the world's estimation, but in your own. The quality of judgment is the most divisive quality that you possess, because it will, at any cost, prove itself to be the better. But all you are really trying to do is make yourself feel *equal*. For if you truly knew yourself to be 'better,' you would manifest compassion, because you would understand that judgment is not a quality that ever heals. *Judgment* does not heal any one, or any thing, at any time. Judgment is the killer. So those who judge against their fellow man have to be responsible for realizing that they are desperately trying to keep their own self-judgment locked up in another area of their life. There is a part of your psyche that doesn't want you to look inward, so it tricks you into looking out there. If you have judgment, you do not have compassion, because they cannot exist together. If you have compassion you cannot judge, because you understand from the point of compassion that the person who is before you in this moment, *can act no differently*. And you *cannot*, impose your rules on them because there is always some part of *your* consciousness that other people can look at and judge to be wrong.

Why is judgment a crucial issue and what does it have to do with energy? Judgment is a killer, because it locks you inside your physical body. When you are in the act of judging, you can feel it in your consciousness and in your body. It is often felt as a heavy weight in the heart center. Lack of love is another expression for judgment. And this lack takes your energy and closes it in upon itself. Energy does two things: it either expands or it contracts. It moves out, or it implodes. When it is imploding through judgment, you are holding inside yourself all the power that if released, would begin to clarify and help you understand whatever difficulty you are in. But you are not capable of this understanding, because you're hanging on to a judgment inside your being which stops the energy from moving through you. This blockage will cause different experiences. You may start losing money, or it will no longer be given to you; your health may decline; friendships or material things may slip from your life. Not all of this at once, but watch what contraction does. You have fewer and fewer people around you, smaller and smaller amounts of energy coming in, and your *life* begins to implode upon itself. It becomes difficult to do even simple things. If just getting up and moving through your day is hard, understand that somewhere in your psyche you have clamped down on your view of yourself because you are afraid. You need not be afraid. You have hundreds of parts to your being, and because one part is in shadow does not mean that you are not a wondrous consciousness. But you have to be aware that you can get in and find out the color, the nature, the content, the feeling, and the shape of your shadow. It has a shape, it has a form, it has a feeling, it is alive, and *it is there*. It is sometimes based on past lives —lives where you have had to undergo tremendous duress, and in order to get through those times, you have had to act within certain, strict formats. That restricted action kept you alive.

Let us speak about some of those times. Let us take stealing, for example. There have been lifetimes when most of you have had to override the law and choose to steal in order to keep people alive, usually those that you were responsible for: children, husbands, wives, whoever it might be. And so, with consciousness you say: "The greater law is to take care of those that I love, the lesser law is the material law." You go along for many lifetimes with this operative belief, and it doesn't bother you. But now it presents itself in this lifetime, and you have, not people stealing oranges and apples, but real estate brokers that lie just a little; businessmen that cheat just a little; house-wives that take money from their husbands just a little; all of these things, just a little. And you see it as no great problem for yourselves. It's just a little, no harm done. But there *is*, harm done because these acts stay inside, quietly eating away at you. So what you do to keep from looking at your shadow is to find somebody else's and see what you can do to make trouble over it. And that can work very well for you. It may be helpful for your friend to hear about *their* shadow from you, or it may not. It is more helpful to realize that every time you find yourself in serious judgment against someone else, it is because there is a hidden judgment about yourself that you do not wish to see.

You have been crying out for a long time for an increase in energy to expand your awareness, and the energy is present *now*. *Now* is the time to pay attention, because you will not be able to participate with this energy in power and beauty until you understand that *judgment* is the killer of your consciousness in this particular decade.

Because of it, you cannot get in touch with your own empowered dynamic wonder and wholeness. Judgment stands there as a shadow between you. And if you wish to risk all to gain all, find out what form your shadow takes. You can do this by *asking your friends*. The wonderful thing is that you are as glass to each other. You see through each other. Because this is a world in which you want to survive, when you feel under attack you have all become very good at scanning each other. You have to know where everyone is, where they are strong, where they are weak, when to attack, if to attack, how to attack. You move in the outside world beautifully, so you know each other well. If you truly want to make that giant step into your shadow and look around at it, ask those who know truly love you to tell you what it is. Do not ask those who profess to love you, for they will tell you what *they* want your shadow to be. Pick the ones that your being knows are trustworthy as friends. They will understand that you are truly open to the desire to see your total being and they will help you. Find those who love you, and tell them that this is the most serious thing you will ever ask of them.

If you have the courage and if you have a handful of trusted and true friends, ask. Ask with the openness of consciousness that will allow you to hear. It will hurt, you will squirm and try to run, but stay and listen. And like a bell ringing in your awareness, you will know if what they say is true, and they will not be able to deceive you. If you are in a state of open, empowered awareness and the words come in, the body will resound to them. It is a physical sensation, and you *will* know the truth of what you hear. You will feel a tightening in the throat, in the solar plexis, in the shoulders. And then, as the physical body takes it in, please open up and breathe. *Don't implode.* Just open up and tell yourself that you are all right. It is time to quit pretending that you are perfect. If you were perfect you would not need to be here. If you had perfect balance in your energy fields, you would be vibrating at such a rate that you would have trouble staying on this earth plane. So please be ready to hear what a loved one can show you about your shadow.

What then, is your situation, if you do not have such a friend, or circle of friends? How do you go about identifying your shadows? Take the warrior's path, the solitary way. You get yourself a large notebook and each day you spend time telling yourself the things about yourself that you have always known to be true, but have rarely had the courage to face. You acknowledge your weaknesses again and again to yourself. And in this process you will gain the strength to be in a position of becoming alive to the jeopardy of moving into those areas of weakness. In that moment, you can call upon other areas of your consciousness, other parts of your being, that are strong and clear, to come to your aid. As you work with this material, day after day, writing it down, you will find that you move from the mental process of writing, to a deep instinctual process of allowing the inner truths about yourself to keep bubbling up. Over and over again, this kind of material comes up and comes out, as it bypasses the mental process. It is simply a way the intuition allows itself to guide you in seeing parts of your being. And it does it in a gentle way. Your being can be trusted. It will not present you with the information before you are ready to receive it. So it will be a gentle stirring up, a gentle coming out, and you will know when truth has been written, because it will ring a bell in the sky of the mind, in the sky of the being which you will hear, and know for truth. And once you have defined the area of weakness, the next step is to find the appropriate solution to living in a new way. How can you re-identify yourself so that the old picture is no longer who you are? This is when the whole world comes back as your mirror. A book will catch your eye, and in it will be information that you can use. You will be talking with someone and they will say something that resounds in your being. Your intuition begins to awaken you through dreams and daydreams.

The minute that you want to find the way out is the minute that you start to find the way out. And be dedicated to looking every day and seeing the way to *your* truth and *your* light.

At the moment of your enlightenment, the person you will bow down to in deepest gratitude is the one who dared to show you your face. Not in some kind of antagonistic, negative way, but in a way that says they love you and are committed to seeing you fly free. They are willing to speak the truth as they feel it about you. I have told you from the beginning that most of you have one remaining, buried root within you, based on different things. It could be arrogance, based on fear; it could be sexuality, based on a need to use others. But understand, that whatever your dark side, it is based upon and has come to life as a defense from another time when it was very appropriate. What is needful now is to reprogram your mechanism.

Let us take sexuality, for instance. There have been times and periods in history when it was an absolute necessity for all of you to be as licentious as you possibly could, because the survival of mankind depended on population. And you had to override personal preferences in order to get the job done. So part of the psyche has a resounding awareness that says, this kind of behavior is best for me and best for the planet. As you look around the earth, this is no longer the case. But the programming is still there. Now you can move sexually in the world in any way you want. The way for you to find out if you are moving appropriately is to listen to what your world has to say to you. If your world says you are acting in painful or inappropriate ways, and you hear that statement over and over again, don't you think you ought to look at it? You have to realize that you are moving out of a part of your psyche that hasn't caught up with the rest of you. And you all have parts to your psyche that haven't caught up with the rest of you.

Let's take another example, the wonderful one called "work ethic." Work and ethic are very limited words. Do you hear the sharpness of the sounds? You can tell how expansive words are by how they sound. Does work ethic sound very expansive? The limitation of that phrase resounds in the world. It moves with a very specific meaning, because there have been lifetimes when it was essential that you put the work ethic first, and personal desire, ease, family, nurturing—second. You are not nasty, terrible people! You are just moving out of patterns that have been resounding through this world for centuries. You have not taken the opportunity to decide which of them are still useful. If your whole world is saying to you that you work too hard, it is possible that you are working out of past experience so ask yourself if it is really worth the price. With *any* of these patterns, ask yourself if it is worth the price. Also, look around and ask your environment. Then get back into your being and decide.

You choose things because of habituated patterns. Habituated patterns are not going to feel very comfortable in the next few years. They are going to be pounded upon relentlessly. You have asked to come to the earth plane at a time when transformation is possible. Transformation is possible now, and it isn't always going to feel good. But either you are a warrior or you are not. You picked this time to return, so you are ready on some level to face these patterns. Ask your environment and the people in it. You do not live in a closed universe. It constantly mirrors the truth back to you. Listen to your children, those of you who dare. Children have the capacity to speak truth without sweetness. They speak it, and *you* hope that it's not true. But that does not mean that you have to believe every negative thing that comes at you. If you *consistently* hear the same message in one form or another, please pay attention. And if you really want to be a warrior, actively start looking for it. By that I mean, you say "Today I will be so open that I will hear the messages about my shadow again and again because I *want to know*." So you move in the world, not with hiding your head in your hands, but with your arms open, and when you make the choice to hear about your shadow, it will not be so painful. When you ,*choose* to hear something about yourself that you do not like, it does not hurt nearly as much as when you are defending yourself against it. Do you understand the difference? Standing there boldly, ready to listen because of your own need to be whole is much different from sticking your chin out and just taking it. When you are defending yourself, you shut down so the information barely trickles through. When a message about your shadow comes in, the first thing you say is, "Let's go out." But the information will come, it must because you are calling it in for your own wholeness.

Do not deceive yourselves, my friends. Part of your world could tell you a falsity, but not all of it. And those of you who are really willing to learn about yourselves, each day will learn one more thing. Those of you that want to be whole, open up and hear. You would not be on the earth plane if you did not have some unfinished business. Finish it up! And you can finish it by knowing yourself totally. The wonderful thing is, once you truly know your weaknesses, the process itself begins to take care of them. I have told you: of yourself, you can do nothing. And I mean it. Address your shadows constantly in your being, and ask the seen and the unseen world for help. This is where prayer is a wonderful device, an ongoing prayer that asks that you be cleared of your shadows, and that you understand clearly what you are doing. When you are alive to the possibility of clearly seeing your shadows, your whole universe comes in and begins to show you the solution. Keep bringing those shadow parts into the light, and eventually they will dissipate. Acknowledge, and keep acknowledging, those parts of you and your desire to change and be different. The minute you put out the call for change, the energy will start coming, and then you just need to receive it. Your whole body will begin to feel different, because you have quit fighting yourself.

Please realize that you've been fighting yourself. Hiding from your shadows is fighting yourself. Being willing to see yourself is being on your own side. My friends, there is no one that is not absolutely capable of finishing with their shadow and you start by acknowledging your unfinished, shadow parts and your desire to be done with them. By doing this, you can become 51% harmless. Do you understand why? When you are concerned with your shadow, it's like having a dog behind your back, nagging at you, pulling at your shirt, and chewing on your pants. It's hard to really be alive and compassionate with the world because you've got this thing behind you that's bothering you, and you are concerned with it. But when you have taken your shadow, placed it in front of you and stated that you wish to know it, then you have a chance of communication, of communion, and of resolution.

In those moments of truly getting into your being and paying attention to your shadow, you become so human that you love the rest of humanity. You have to be human yourself to love mankind. Otherwise you stand above it, and you cannot love from above. How do you think those Enlightened Ones love? The roots of their power go deeply into the depths of the blue space beneath this planet, and their heads fly with the stars so high that your eyes cannot perceive them. Do you think that they love from above you only? Their beings are so vast that they hold this entire createdness in one hand. They do not love from above, from a superior stance, they love from their wholeness. And *your* being is *that* vast, you have just forgotten. You think yourself to be a little person walking on a little planet. That is not so. *Your* heads are in the stars and your feet drop into deep blue space. *That* is how vast you are! You don't need to be rescued, you don't need to be saved. You are the rescuer and you are the saved. All you have to do is to wake up! And 'waking up' means taking everything behind you that you have tried to hide from and placing it in your vision. Sleepers hide from themselves. The warrior awakens and says, "I am ready. I want to know, so I can be harmless. I want to be harmless, because it is the only way to move in power on this planet." When you are one with humanity and have not placed yourself above it, tears of compassion will flow and you won't be able to see anything but the One. *There is only One.* Your bodies have taken that one light and splintered it off into millions of lights. But the sun moving through a prism does not lose its original oneness. And that is what you are. When you are willing to face your unfinished business, your heart will break open, and you will see that all of you suffer from the same problem. You are afraid, because you have misidentified yourselves, and think that you are a small entity, moving through a perilous world to an unknown end.

What you are going to know when the Oneness is before you, is that everything past what your eyes can see is who you are, and none of it can hurt you. And you will know that you have always walked in total safety. There has not been one moment since you put your feet on this planet that you were not utterly safe. How could a being so vast as you, have fear of your smallness? It is not possible. You have just forgotten who you really are. Wake up! Every morning and every moment of the day that you can, remember who you are. Remember the stars of your mind and the power of your feet. And every moment that you touch that vastness, you will bring it that much more into your consciousness, and you will begin to feel it as surely as the limitations you now feel. But you have to remember, and *that's all* you have to remember. You cannot create those vast beings of consciousness, and you don't need to, because that is who you are. You have taken limitation as *small* as it can go. In the remembrance comes the reawakening. *It will happen!* Wake up, we need you.

THE PATH

Transformation is not a process—it is a willingness.

Living out of the Moment

Opening the Heart

Meditation as a Guide to Inner Awareness

The Message of St. Francis

The Comforter

LIVING OUT OF THE MOMENT
11 March 1979
Socorro, New Mexico

Q: Would you comment on your seemingly contradictory statements that "It is helpful to have a guru," and "Do not give your power to anyone else"?

This is a valid question, for I have stated that you need a higher power in order to help you to awaken and I have also stated that you should never give your power away. So how do these statements relate to each other? First, let us be clear on what we mean by 'power': I am referring to that inner feeling of strength and expansion that manifests in the world as action that is both maximum for the individual and harmless to others. What you must understand is that if you are dealing with a real guru or teacher on the earth plane, the question will never arise, because the guru has absolutely no desire to take anything from you. In truth, he wants to share all of himself with you. The guru is in a state of having no ego self to give to you, so no ego self to take from you. When I tell you not to give your power to others, I am being very specific. If you have a teacher or a guru who in some way wants something from you, or demands that you come to them with all of your very small and trivial problems, then I would ask you to look at that relationship again. All it does is give you a feeling of being weak and unable to cope with your own situations, when indeed, the opposite is really true. You are *totally* able to cope, and it is precisely the illusion that you are *not*, that I am trying to break. So, those of you in relationships with teachers, gurus, or masters, look carefully, because they should be turning your mundane questions back on you. The basic issue is always *how to awaken*? Any other is not of lasting importance.

When you place a limited question before a teacher, you are giving value to the problem that you are presenting, and in answering you, the teacher is agreeing that such things are important. This weakens rather than strengthens you. The true teacher wants to eat away at your illusions, not shore up your sagging bridge of unreality. Answering limited questions strengthens your belief in the importance of such questions, and a true teacher wants you to awaken to who you really are.

When you surrender to the highest awareness that you can conceive of, you are not giving your power away, for what happens is a mingling of your power with that of 'the other.' In truth, these two seemingly separated 'Powers' have always been joined. *All* Divine energies are already joined, without any act of surrender of any kind. My job is to awaken you to the fact that you *can use* this truth. So, when I speak of 'surrender,' it is not a giving up of power, but a joining of powers. You do not feel a weakening, but an incredibly powerful strengthening inside your being. The hallmark that you have touched upon real Divine Energy is *a rush of power*! And I don't mean arrogance, I mean power that moves through your being, uplifts, that is a bold, courageous, on-going feeling of *rightness. That* is the hallmark of having connected with the Divine Source. If you feel insignificant and weak, then I think whatever you are doing is not 'surrender'! Have I made this clear? It IS an important point.

If your guru or teacher makes you feel impotent and helpless, look again at what you have committed to. It is the disciple's responsibility to analyze the relationship that they have with any teacher, either on the earth plane or on other planes. It is also the disciple's responsibility to be watching carefully how that relationship is going. If that relationship is turning into one of utter dependance for the minutiae of life, or even the minutiae of one's spiritual life, then I think you must question the source. On the other hand, if you are constantly being turned back on yourself to develop your own inner strengths, to discover what awareness can really be, then I would say that you are in the vibrational pattern of a true teacher. When you learn to help yourself, you will know that you are really dropping the 'unreal,' and that many things within you are undergoing the change of a new birth, a new opening, and a new awakening.

Q: Would you speak about the difference between 'detach ment' and 'surrender'?

Ultimately, when you reach the end of either road, you will see that both have led to the same point, and that there never was much difference between detachment and surrender to begin with. The differences are in the nature of the person who is attempting to be either detached or surrendered in their life. Since people's basic strengths lie in different areas, detachment may be the most important factor to some, and to others, surrender is the key. The person who feels that the love quality is of maximum importance is the one who will speak in terms of surrender, because you surrender *to* something. So, you will surrender in stages to whatever is most powerful for you. That is where the gurus and different avatars can be the most help. For those who don't feel attracted to any kind of personalized deity, or real guru, surrendering to God is the option. But don't forget the main substructure upon which all of these different 'dieties' are built: *there is only the One*, and a real awareness of this is possible.

The other path is the way of detachment. This is for the type of person who we could call the 'intellectual.' In surrender, the emotional body is the one that is used to make the thrust toward Freedom. In detachment, it is the 'mental body' that is used. Some people are more interested in and act out of their emotions, while others act more from the mind. In detachment you watch mind and emotion play out their different roles so that in the end you will be able to see that *your* role on the earth plane is *not* who you are. To practice detachment, you have to observe yourself, and you have to do it critically. Critically in the sense of honesty and integrity, with the clarity to make sure what it is that you are observing in yourself. Do not over-praise or over-condemn yourself, but stick to the real truth of the situation. You will often find that the people around you will let you know where you stand in many situations. If you listen carefully to what other people say to you, then watch your responses to them, you will get definite indications of where you are out of balance. These are not things to worry about, just look within your being, find out where you stand, and without any great fanfare or over-concern, go about the business of straightening it out. You can understand how this works in one day of critical observation! It is not mysterious. *Pay attention*, then *practice* what you have learned. If you find that you are using your intellectual faculty too much, make a conscious decision that you are going to put it on hold and use something else. Go within and *feel out* the problem. And if you are one of those who is always emotional, then put that response aside and use your *reasoning* faculty to deal with the problem.As you go the way of detachment, also keep as a constant companion the knowledge that Love is absolutely crucial. And if you have decided that your way is surrender of the heart, know that you must keep with you the companion faculty of Reason. They *must* go together to be balanced. And in the balance and harmony of the continuing search, you will find a definite pattern of slow, constant unfoldment.

Q:Why does balance seem to be important?

Most people are in an incarnative pattern in order to balance energies because unbalanced energies will continue to harass you. Emotional, mental, or physical imbalances rise up to cause confusion and to cloud simple issues. Some people may have a great deal of love quality, but they may also become despondent or agitated too easily. It would help them to use the logical faculty that comes from the intellect, in order to 'quiet' these energies down. And conversely, there are many intellectuals who are so heavily weighted in the mental area that their intuitive faculties are no longer available to them, and they need to get in touch with the emotional side of their being, so that the balance can be brought about.

It is easier to make a serious thrust toward Freedom when you are not hampered by a serious lack of balance. If you are almost always using either your mental or emotional faculties, one over the other, then you may know that you are imbalanced. You are even encouraged to do this today because of the prevalent belief that the male has the intellectual personality, and the female the emotional. This belief structure keeps you from allowing yourself to move easily from one area to the other. The well-balanced person has both of these qualities in hand and is able to love with a deep and understanding heart and can at the same time be detached from too much emotion or too much intellect.

Q:How can we practice the quality of detachment?

Let us use an example. Take a situation that is common on the earth plane today—that of driving a car in traffic. You have done a full day's work and are on your way home, surrounded by many cars. You are very tired, and you know that it will take a long time to get home because of the heavy traffic. Someone in front of you starts to drive in an erratic manner (erratic being any way other than how you think they should drive). Now you have an opportunity to learn detachment! The first thing that you will feel is a rush of resentment. There is a definite movement of anger within the body form. In the beginning stages of this process, you will not be able to stop that first rush of anger—and that is all right. But the second thing you do is very important. *The minute you feel it*, you say, "This is anger!"*Name* the emotion in your mind: "This is *anger*!" What you want to make clear is that there is anger, and there is *someone* who is in the *state* of anger. Do not say, "I am angry," which would make you one with it, but "This is anger," which makes it two. The next step is to *make your decision*. And you will soon discover that you *can* make a decision. This can point the way to detachment.

117

If your responses were a force over which you had no control, you would not be able to make any decisions about them at all. They would control you, and you would end up as some kind of unaware receptacle for whatever emotion decides to move through you. But you will quickly find that you and the emotion *are not* one, and it is at this stage that you choose. Do you want to play the same tape of anger over again? You know how it goes; you try to out-manipulate the other car, you blow your horn, make obscene gestures, yell and scream—this is all part of it! You try to 'get even,' sometimes even perhaps hurting yourself and your own vehicle in order to get revenge. Eventually, you will discover that it doesn't really matter whether or not you get angry at the other person, because that is not the real issue. If you wish to be Free, you must recognize that your power lies with your choices. *At that instant*, you can choose another response.

Notice that an energy rises up within you, *recognize* the energy, then *name* the emotion. In the naming can often come the freeing, because you have already moved the response one step away from you. Then, you must *desire* to change that response. *And so you can*! You begin by simply saying, "I choose differently *Now*!" So, choose. It is not hard to experience detachment. But what *is* hard, my friends, is to decide that you want to experience detachment. Because if you are being very honest, you will find that when you are 'attacked,' you want to get even! You want to harbor thoughts of resentment, of how to 'pay back' what you think has been given to you. You will also find nobody to stop you, so go on and attack. But in the process you will learn that it is *you* who ends up hurting and you will see that this is a very boring way to live your life. You will find that creative results are much more enlivening than anger and rebuttal. You *are* co-creators with God, and you might as well get on with the job of co-creating in a way that will be eternal and uplifting and joyful, and forget about the ways that are so limiting, hostile and negative towards others.

So be totally within yourself. Be grounded with what is happening in that moment. When you are driving the car, be aware of your hand on the wheel, your foot on the pedal, the feel of wind around your head, the smell of the air. Be in touch with all of this, so when the anger and resentment arise, you will *be there*. You will not have to come back from some fantasy about a conversation you wish you had with your boss. In the moment you can feel the emotion and recognize it, so you have the opportunity to make changes, and thereby detach yourself from the same old responses. If your attention is not in the present it will make the job very difficult, because the emotion and your response will come over you so quickly that you will react in the same old way. All of these things happen quickly. That is why you can be freed in an instant, or caught in an instant! And so, to create the opportunity to be free, you have to *be where you are* every moment.

Q: Would you tell us how to be free from attachments to other things, such as objects or desires?

A very good question. I think you have to start with the ones that come to you the most, and are the easiest to touch upon. When you find out what they are, ask yourself *why* you want to detach from them. It is vital for you to believe that it is *important* and *valid* for you to detach from whatever desire it is. As long as you feel that there is some value in being attached to a person, an object, or a cause, you will not want to be free of it. You cannot fight against yourself. You cannot detach from something you still want to be attached to. So, first of all, face the fact that you have a particular attachment. Pick out one that is strong. It could be your mate, or money, or power, or sex, or alcohol, or drugs; it could be many things. So, write out a list of what it is that you get by being attached. What is it that you fear will happen if this attachment is removed from you?

For instance, let us take the example of a relationship. People operate under the illusion that if you are greatly attached to someone, it is somehow a positive aspect of being. But that depends very much on *how* you are attached. If you are attached through love, that is one thing; but if you are attached through fear, that is something else again. Many relationships are based on fear; fear of loss. Ask yourself what would happen if your mate were to leave your life. Look at it from this angle, and you will see where this relationship stands in meaning to you. Does it mean that without this mate, you are not lovable? That you will never find another person to love you—that you will be alone? People who have a definite attachment to another person, and loose that person, are often overwhelmed by a feeling of not being lovable. They have placed their belief in their own value in the hands of another person. This is extremely foolish and also extremely unrealistic. When you look at your relationship, and realize that you are attached, you will see that you have involved yourself in something that is limiting. Then you will see it, not as a positive, but as a negative aspect of your life, and you can throw all of your weight behind your sedire to be free of it. Be free of the attachment, and continue to build on the limitless Love. It's much more satisfying! Keep the relationship but let go of the possession.

Let us then talk about those who are attached to material objects, let's say a car. You may think that this type of attachment is not really a problem, but that depends. It depends on what that car or object means to you. To the person that is very materialistic, the car can mean that they see themselves as valuable in the light of their possessions. This is the measure of their worth. It doesn't matter if you are attached to a car, or a person. If you are being attached to something outside of yourself, you will feel that you are much less without it. And when you do see your attachments, you don't walk out on your love relationships, and you don't sell all of your possessions. What you do is recognize that behind the attachment is a feeling of emptiness, of separateness, of vacancy. And trying to attach yourself to someone or something to fill that vacancy is not a healthy and freeing way to live your life. With that realization, you will have begun the process of detachment. Seeing value in letting go of your attachments is the first step.

Now you are moving in harmony with your own deepest and true desire, which is to be Free. You may keep on building the illusion of separateness like children building bridges of sand along the seashore. It can be fun, but should not be taken very seriously. This is a good way of looking at all of your attachments, that they are fun, and they can be helpful, but they should not be taken so seriously. Do not take your love affairs so seriously that all else pales beside them. Neither should you let your materialistic life become so serious that you cannot see that loss of your possessions would be acceptable. Allow these things to move naturally in and out of your life, and participate with them with joy and interest. Once you have seen the necessity for detachment, you have joined your will with the Divine Will, and the process becomes easier.

The next step is to use *awareness* as your greatest tool. With awareness, you remind yourself who you are. And detachment is a way of remembering, and surrender is a way of remembering. They are ways to remind you, so that you can begin to free yourself from the illusion of what you are not. As long as you think things are worth having, worth relating to, worth your deepest energy, *you will never detach*! Because it is what you desire most that will manifest; and until you get in touch with that deep desire of wanting to be Free, you will continue to follow the ego-projection that rests on the idea of separateness. To say that one relationship is more important than another is to deny that all is One. The ego creates special relationships in order to convince you that you are indeed separate and therefore special. But the fact is that you are *all the same*. You always have been, and you always will be; from the very loftiest to the most degenerate. *You are all the same*! And all of your little differences are illusions that you hold to keep you in bondage. Do not give them another thought, they are not important. Let them sink back into the nothingness from which they arose, and stand confident that in this moment is the totality of the One, and it is *only in this moment* that you can touch that Totality!

121

Q: It seems that eliminating desire consists primarily of paying attention to our desires. Is paying attention practicing detachment and surrender?

Therein does lie the answer because you can only pay attention in the moment. It is so simple! When you are in the moment, *you are there*, and all of the rest is not there. Separateness cannot exist in the moment! There is just you and what surrounds you and is in you, and if you are paying attention, you will know exactly what that is. So, in the end, *attention* is the key. How then does one think of surrender, in terms of paying attention? Well, what are you surrendering TO? You surrender to the One God in that moment. You don't surrender once and then forget about it. Surrender is that quality of *being* that stays tuned each moment to the Vastness. And, in order to stay attuned to the Vastness, you have to be where the Vastness is! And where is that? It is *here*. Because there is no such thing as 'future' and 'past,' there is only the *now*! And you have to be here, in order to participate in it.

When people want to control other people or events or even their own emotions, they have to rely on past events or future desires. Don't try to control. *Allow*! And, in the allowing will come the peace, knowledge, and Freedom of the moment, because what is before you now is the only thing you can truly know. It is being born, it is dying, and it is everything in between. All of the Wholeness is simply the continuation of the moment and that is *all* that it is!

OPENING THE HEART
11 November 1980
Socorro, New Mexico

Bartholomew's blessing to newlywed Stephen and Katherine:

You, as well as others, have felt the desire to love more, but also realize the limitations of the moment. There is a wish to expand one's own love and transform relationships into fit vehicles for one's self, each other and the Divine to act through. And so tonight, in honor of your marriage, I would like to say one thing. Whatever standards you might hold on the physical plane, in the eyes of the Divine, there is only one standard to hold to in your consciousness, each for the other. Can you both, as you look at each other, see with the power of the Golden Light? Can you always remember, no matter what should pass between you, that the Light is present and it is there for each of you to share in ever-increasing abundance? Should you ever doubt, please remember this: if you choose to love, you love with that Light, and never with your limited mind. You always love with that Light and it is my promise to you that it does exist in each of you. I ask you to hold that existence forevermore; because as you, Katherine, see that Light in him, and Stephen in Katherine, you will come to understand who you are, who the other is and what in the end all of the Createdness is. Hold to this one standard in your hearts and you cannot fail. You may stumble many times and in many ways, but if you hold that view each for the other you cannot fail, because this standard promises always to try again. There is no such thing as failure in Love, only the recognition of the desire to try again and again and yet again.

Beginning thus, may we then extend to what I feel is a most important question. How can you with the desire to love more, but in view of the limitations of your understanding of love, accomplish that goal?

One of the problems with the spiritual quest is that it can become so intellectual that the one quality that will help you the most is lost. That quality is the ability to love. Many come to me and say they want to love but don't know how, so I would now like to share with you some of my observations of mankind. In this time of mentalization, of concepts and ideas, man is forgetting something very simple. What you are forgetting is that *the basic quality of man's consciousness is Love*. The ever-shifting shadows that play upon the surface of that Love are really nothing more than shadows, but since you have taken them to be reality, the play engrosses you and the love eludes you. Man therefore says he doesn't know how to love. You *do* know how to love, but when you believe that you do not know how to go about it, then you have to be taught. This is the era of 'having to be taught' everything. And now you have to be taught to love. Nonsense! Who will you find to teach you? Let us say that you have found someone you feel is capable of love and you ask him to explain how he became so loving. A really loving person rarely sees himself as loving, so he will be unable to offer any explanations or instructions. Therefore you cannot go to someone who is loving to tell you how to love, for he will say that he has no idea how he does it. But if you go to someone who is not loving, he will readily tell you how. And he will give you a regimen to follow to attain it. It will take many books and involve many techniques, and when you are finished and have paid your money, the question will still remain. Are you any closer to learning how to love?

No one needs to learn how to love. What is necessary is something far easier, which is to drop your fears. When your fear is gone, love is present. Love and fear cannot exist together. You cannot stir up a pot of love and serve it. It is a 'commodity' that is always with you. But fear takes your natural feelings and squeezes them and if they are squeezed long enough and hard enough, you come to a place where the very thought of giving love causes constriction in the body—in the throat, chest, or stomach. You yearn to say something loving, but you tighten up. This is fear. It is not that you are basically an unloving person. I have never seen anyone who is not loving, just as I have never seen anyone who is not courageous. There is a fear that if you give out love, the other person will reject it. How does this fear begin? Just look at the children. This world is not set up for the benefit of children, it is a very difficult world for children to grow up in. There was a time when it was much easier to be spontaneously loving, because there was time for love. Now there is a lot of time for sex, but no time for love. Love takes time. One needs to start very young, and if you are so busy you cannot show love for the young, they will grow up and find no time for love either.

What can be done? You are adults, and cannot return to your childhood. You who feel incapable of love, please remember that there is no one now or ever who is *incapable* of love. There are those of you who are afraid to love, but no one that has no love. Not only are you capable of love, but you are capable of tremendous love. There is nothing so wonderful as loving! But the first thing needed is to see yourself differently. Do not view yourself as some little worm scrambling for love but as a full-blown, wondrously open being, filled with abiding love. And you may not consciously feel or know about that, so we will devise a technique to show you.

When you meditate, those of you who do meditate, I think it important that you concentrate on the center which you call the heart center (the area of the heart). Do not make the mistake of thinking that you have no energy going into that center, but rather be willing to experience the reality of something moving there. The quieter you get in your meditation, the more you will experience a feeling in the heart center and if you are paying attention you will begin to sense just a little warmth. The movement is experienced there as heat energy. And when this energy begins to warm you a little, then you will know that the heart center is coming into your consciousness.

For those of you who do not meditate, what then? It is a little more difficult. You must start to realize that you are a loving person.

127

Most people think that loving someone means being nicer to them, or more glamorous, more agreeable, or whatever. That belief places you in a very vulnerable position, for all of those ways of 'loving' come from outside of you, and if you are depending on outside things to make people love you, you will fail. Of course you can start being kinder. I do recommend that. It is not easy for others to love someone who is being unkind or inconsiderate, or who continuously says nasty things and is a real problem! So you have to start believing that *you are a loving person*. People sit before me and tell me over and over that they are not loving and every time you say you are not loving, you are that much further from being loving. You begin to love by being aware of the heart center and realizing that it is the point from which love energy flows. It does not flow from your head or your toe, but from the heart. Rest there more and more instead of in your mind with all of its concerns and fantasies. It is not hard. We are talking about that moving energy which is love; sparkling, wonderful Love.

But please, do not ask to generate that love for a particular person unless that person be yourself. Do not decide that you are determined to 'love George.' It will not work, for you will create a separation; yourself and George. Then you will have to *do* something with George. Maybe George doesn't want your love. Maybe George would just as soon have you love Harry. So, don't be particular about it, just be open to Love. Start that energy into motion and when you start the love energy flowing, a wonderful thing will happen. *You will start to love yourself*! Isn't that terrible, you start to love yourself. Your chest expands a little, your walk is a little bouncier, you feel a little more alive. If others say things to you that are not pleasing, somehow it doesn't matter because you have begun to build the power of that energy within you. Do not think about where it will be placed, only be concerned with generating it. Where it goes is its own business. When someone tells me they love others but not themselves, I do not believe them. You cannot love 'out there' if you do not have love 'in here.' So then, what is love?

A most important question. There is a feeling called 'love' that is an emotion which comes and goes. When you are feeling good, you are loving; when you are feeling grumpy, you are not. That is not the kind of love I am talking about. I am referring to an observable energy field in the Vastness. It is radiant pink and it moves and flows and sparkles. It moves through you and it feels wonderful. And as it moves, it selects that which is now called the 'heart center' or 'heart chakra' to move through and go where it will. The fact is, love is not something that you churn around in your mind or move with your emotional body or turn off and on. Love is an undulating energy that moves through you, within you and radiates out of you and changes everything. All of the colors of the spectrum are contained within your physical frame. Each one of your chakras radiates a different color, just as a prism creates and radiates the spectrum. They all carry different qualities. Man is ablaze with all of them, not one preferred over another, but all moving, dynamic, alive, and pulsating.

Tonight we are speaking of Love because we are moving into the season of Love. Christmas usually ends with sorrow because you have hoped that the love which the Christ personifies would come alive in you that day. But the day ends and the gifts have not done it, the turkey has not done it and the friends have not done it, because the energy has not been recognized. It does not need to end like that. Starting this day, love energy can be recognized. But it has to begin with a conscious effort. You have to make up your mind. Are you going to concentrate on love or are you going to start to mentalize about it and about how unloving or unlovable you are? What kind of person you think you are is quite irrelevant. Any person at any time can begin to feel this energy, build with it, move with it, and change with it.

I would be delighted to have you try an experiment. Quiet yourself and concentrate intently on the color pink. See it dynamically filling your heart center and be with that glow. When you are walking, feel it; when you are sitting, feel it; when you are talking, feel it; *just feel it*. Snuggle with it. Feel wonderful about it. And all of a sudden you will start to come alive. I mean literally start to come alive and you will begin to sparkle, to feel good! Then perhaps you will become worried because you have no worries. You will get up in the morning feeling happy. Someone will come to you with a problem and you will tell them it is going to be all right. And they will tell you that you do not understand the problem but you will. The power of Love knows that everything can be made wonderfully acceptable. That does not mean all things will change and be pleasant and perfect or that all will go according to your plans. But the Love which is flowing through you will make everything feel very 'right.' When there is dis-ease in your life, it is almost always because you are not loving. When there is physical or mental dis-ease in your life, it comes from agitation and agitated feelings come from not being in harmony with someone—and that someone is yourself. You live most of your days in worry, always waiting for that other shoe to drop on your head. Someone is sure to come along and ruin your day. Someone is sure to hurt your feelings or say something you don't like. You are going to do something that will fail or something that will turn into a mess. All of that may be true—but it does not matter. You can tell yourself that you are going to begin this process of revitalization, then let things go on their own way until such time as you become alive and care about yourself. Do not keep your attention on all of those outer things. This feeling of love has not already happened because you haven't really tried to make it happen. It is simple to love and difficult not to love. Love is natural and when you try to fight against your natural state, it takes energy. So just put all of your problems on hold. There is no one without some degree of anxiety, it is the human situation. But please put that on the back burner and leave it. Start feeling the movement of love, and when your view of things and people around you starts changing, you will be happy. But most of all you will be grateful that you yourself have moved into the space that radiates that Power. It will not matter if others love you, because *you are Loving*. Then others will no longer have to dance to your tune. They can be as they wish to be, free, wonderful, alive and you can allow them to be thus, for you will have no fear. People hang onto each other because they fear that they will lose love, but you will find that you cannot lose love. If it is moving through you, who can take it? The more you give, the more you have.

Love is not an un-natural state for man. It is un-natural when you try to make others love you. That is not the way, my friends; it is not their responsibility to love you. It is your responsibility *to love yourself.* And I do not mean arrogantly. The ego would love you to feel that you are being arrogant by loving yourself. But you cannot love anyone else until you love yourself. You can act loving; yes. You can change yourself from red to green to orange to purple to please other people and you will seem to be loving. But when they want you to be black when you wish to be green, what then? Where then is the love? Love is something within you which flows out as a flood, and the magic that comes others can enjoy. Then, at that time, a paradox—you don't care. There is as much love when you are alone in your home as when it is filled with people. It doesn't matter, for Love is within you and so Love is everywhere you are. If others are there to share, fine. If nobody is there, fine. Love goes on. You love the plants, the rocks, whatever. No anxiety, no frustrations, no demands, *no expectations!* What is there to expect? The purpose of expectations is manipulation. Expectations say, "Meet *my* demands." But Love says, "Meet your own demands; I am content and whole, and will share with you everything that I have. If you want it, take it; if you don't, leave it. I am Love; with no expectations."

That reality is not a dream, it is not a fantasy. It is a possibility and it is possible now. *And it is not hard to do.* It is only a matter of how much time you will spend watching for it. You can either participate in Love, already abundantly present, or you can spend your time worrying about the lack of it. It is your choice. But I tell you this: no one who walks the earth plane is incapable of love. If you enjoy seeing yourself as 'unloving' and if you have identified yourself as an unloving person, you will have to change to see yourself as a loving person. That is difficult, because all of your games have been set up to see yourself as unloving. Be aware of what kind of view of yourself propels you. Do you see yourself as strong, dynamic, capable, loving, intelligent, humorous? No. Why not? All of those qualities are available to you. Do you see yourself as self-pitying, worried, anxious, nervous, neurotic? Yes? Parents say such things to their children and when they keep telling them how weak they are, the children begin to believe it and become exactly what they have heard. There is no reality in those words of weakness. You are confused because you do not know that you are energy in motion. The human is made up of bands of energy in motion, and one of those bands is called *Love*. Activate it, and love yourself. Leave it inert, and nothing changes.

I repeat, do not begin by choosing someone out there that you are determined to 'love.' The person you have to be determined to love is yourself. I am not speaking of your ego-attributes, for they may not be lovable at all. Not everyone who is loved is really a wonderful person. The ego attributes are not the real you and people who are willing can see right through them to the reality of the Love underneath. The physical, mental, and emotional attributes go on. I am not asking you to love your ego, I am asking you to love your Self, your deep Self. Once you start to taste that love and relate to it in an intimate way, you will start accepting those ego parts of you, without identifying with them. And when that happens, you are no longer burdened with problems.

Q: Is there some mantram or statement that we could use to help this process along?

I will not give you any mantrams, for within yourself you will find one that is meaningful. If you come up with one out of your own being it will be relevant. If I give you one, it will be a mentalization. I am in favor of anything that works. The problem with words, however, is that they can become a mental exercise rather than an experiential process. Love is something that you *feel* in the heart. It has nothing to do with your emotional body and does not feel like an emotion. When you feel it, you will know it. You are nothing more or less than energy generators. The kind of energy you generate is up to you. Since you know you are generators, why not generate for your own benefit? Most of you go on automatic and generate whatever comes along. If *you* are not going to control what is generated, the world around you will determine the kind of energy you put out. When you become serious about this process of generating Power, you will want to decide what kind of energy to produce. If it helps to use words, fine. But make sure that the energy is moving and that you feel it. Mentalizing a mantram will only put you to sleep. It has to be something that is alive, and to whatever extent you can use words to be alive, I would recommend them.

To be very honest with you, I think that the greatest help is to go within and start to feel the love that is there. It is quiet, it is subtle, but the more you look for it, the more it will show its face. You find what you look for. It will become warm and when you get this energy moving fast enough, you may begin to feel hot. Don't panic! Don't think you need a cold shower. Don't worry about it. When it happens, let it happen. It will take its own way, and if it should move up and out of you, let it move. You are a generating station, and love is a very obvious and useful energy field to generate. Most of you spend a lot of your time generating fear, doubt, lack, remorse, anger, resentment, self-pity. I would suggest to you that this is not very creative. Instead of trying to change your mate, your children, your boss, or your job, just begin to generate that feeling of love within you. And you can do it! If you do not try it, you will never experience it. Will you wait for prince or princess charming to fall into your lap to do it for you? How many of you have already had a prince or princess charming in their life and had it not work anyway? It does not work because they are outside of you and the love is within.

Q: Since our true nature is Love, have we experienced it but misidentified it?

What happens is that you feel it spontaneously, but then use your intellect to analyze it and try to find the reason for it. You believe that there must be something or someone outside yourself that has caused the feeling. This is where people become addicted to other people. In love affairs you become addicted to the person for whom you have this feeling. The person was in your life and you felt love, so you think that without this person you will never have the feeling again. Be grateful to that person, then keep going. Keep building. Don't rely on others to make you feel more loving; that is your job. When the energy is there, it is wonderful. Most love affairs and marriages begin this way. A wonderful, enraptured feeling! But where does it go? You lose it because you have given to another the responsibility of continuing to generate this feeling in you. So, if that person does not prove satisfactory, you try another. And you have that wonderful feeling again, but soon that one fails and you try another. How many people are you going to go through before you get bored? It is not because there is anything wrong, but because you have relied on someone else to do your work—which is to begin and continue to build the power of love. Do not think or worry about it, do not characterize it, but just *feel* it. It will be in your heart. Stay within your own being and snuggle up to the wonderful feeling within you. Sometimes you laugh, sometimes you weep, and sometimes you just can't speak for it is so wonderful. And it all begins within you. I am not saying that you don't now love people, but I am saying that you must not make other people responsible for the continuation of that feeling within you. It is your responsibility and all it takes is an inner resolve to feel it and to generate it.

Love manifests two physical things. It has a feeling, and surprisingly, it has a fragrance. Many of you who meditate deeply may at times be overwhelmed with various fragrances, such as roses, or violets, or an unknown scent. One woman who once smelled it hunted all over the house for the incense which she thought must be there; she could not believe that it was a spontaneous aroma. Many of the great Avatars carried a fragrance. If you are deeply aware within yourself, it sometimes may come over you, and it smells like a flower. The Energy has substance and at times, because you are in some ways quite child-like and need encouragement, we give you a gift. Such a gift is a fragrance, one that you know to be other-worldly. This brings a great feeling of gratitude. The signs that come to you as a flash of light, a vision, a moment of understanding, a change in your visual field, whatever it might be, are our gifts to encourage you to go on. Please, walk on! We understand how difficult it is to pursue the unseen; how difficult to live for the unseen. So we give gifts that we feel will encourage you. Sometimes we even send 'spooks' (such as myself) to talk with you, hoping that you will be encouraged. So walk on, don't stop. And in the walking comes the courage, comes the faith, comes the experience that transcends thought. Then nothing that anyone can say will turn you back. The one commodity that is ever present is our love for you. This is something you tend to forget and so I would like to tell you again. It is absolutely irrelevant what you do or say, what actions you perform, our love never ceases, our love is ever-present, and could never, ever, leave you! To test it, go within yourself and find out if there is something within you that is alive, that carries a feeling that you call 'Love.' You will not be disappointed. Please, don't try to love someone else. Just become alive with your own love, and there will be many 'someones.' Remember that. You love yourself, and I love myself, so we love each other. The wonder is, that it is all the same.

Q: Can Love be 'documented?'

Man seems unable to understand that his body and his mind are only a very small part of the totality of what he is. So, he places limits on his experiences. Once you get into the movement of the love within you and begin to understand that it is like a river, then you will start to know that all of those limiting ideas can be washed away. The power of Love is a movement, as of a river that floods through you, transforming you, and moving on. *It is not something that you bring into being.*

Some of you seem to think that the power of love depends on whether or not the body is in balance and that they must have a purifying regimen that has to be followed before love can flow. Wonderful—do all the yoga you want, transform your diet, your thoughts, your emotions; do all of that. But if you are saying that you cannot love until you have gone through all of this ritual, you will never love, for there will always be some other transformation needed. There will always be a kidney that needs to be flushed, or a liver mended, or a new herb that is needed to be taken in to do this or that. You will never be in balance, you will be forever making changes. Some of you even say that it cannot be done in the physical but that you must wait until death to love. Those are all limitations. *There is nothing you have to do*! Nothing you have to change or become. Just be snuggly and cozy with what you already are. And that is the kind of thing that science hates and does not understand. The very power of your Awareness, of your becoming familiar with feeling this Energy, builds so much that it begins to move and then to flood. There is an unfortunate trend in the so-called 'spiritual community' that says you have to keep doing things in order to be more receptive to Divine Light, or Divine Love. It is far harder to transform your body than it is to start Love moving in your heart. The amount of love doesn't depend on your physical vehicle. Did St. Francis have a healthy, dynamic body? Quite the contrary; he was a living wreck. He didn't sleep and he didn't eat the right foods. Do you think his hormonal balance was up to par? That the spit test would decide if his kidneys were properly functioning? That his mineral balance was complete? What are you talking about? You are making excuses for delaying and waiting. There is only one thing he did, and he did it all day and all night. He just kept saying, "God, make me loving." He did not say, "Make them love me," but, "Let me love!" And they took him up on it and they will take you up on it, too. You do not need to have a balanced aura, or a clean kidney. All you need is the humility to say, "I want to Love, and I don't care if anyone loves me." It will start, it will grow and you will cry, without knowing why. Do not make excuses, nor let others make excuses for you. You do not need anything to be totally loving, except the desire to be loving. And no human being lacks that quality. However much it might be hidden, it is not gone. Man innately knows that his road to the Light is through Love. More than anything else, man wants to go Home, and it is on the wings of love that you fly Home! Please, don't postpone it.

MEDITATION AS A GUIDE
TO INNER AWARENESS
24 January 1982
Albuquerque, New Mexico

Q: Will you speak about some of the unusual symptoms that accompany the practice of meditation?

I discuss this with some degree of trepidation because of the vast cornucopia of possibilities. My fear is that you will feel you have failed as a seeker if none of these responses that we speak of has happened to you. I would like to begin by stating that none of the signs of Enlightenment or Understanding have to come in these ways. We must also admit and acknowledge that for some persons their physical apparatus does respond easily to deep meditation. Through moment-to-moment intensive self-searching in times of emotional difficulties, certain manifestations do sometimes occur. So perhaps we can point out ways in which they may be made useful to you.

Oftentimes, the body responds to an intake of energy and if you are on any kind of true inner Quest, almost imperceptibly your physical body will begin to change. Many who go into deep meditation find as a by-product that a difficult physical condition has improved. When you acknowledge, even on a superficial level, that you are moving energy, you will come to the understanding that you are surrounded by vast fields of different types of undulating energy. In most cases you cannot see this with your eyes or hear it with your ears, but occasionally you may feel it in your body.

Why should you meditate, when so many of you find it such a bore? If that is the case, don't meditate, but do find some way to allow those Energies to start moving. There are many ways to do this. Spiritual dancing is one because, in the process of letting go to the flood of motion and sound, there is a possibility of dropping your old way of seeing things, even if only for a short while. Most of the time you see with your mind, not with your eyes. The trouble with seeing with your mind is that you become addicted to the same kinds of 'mentalizations.' You see yourself as a woman, a mother, a wife, a businessperson, etc. This is who you think you are. If there is some trauma, for example, your child dies, or your mate leaves you, you become afraid. The fear comes because one view of yourself is now gone. You are no longer a wife. If you are not a wife, *who are you*? The mind and the ego strive to fill that gap as quickly as possible, providing another view of yourself so that you won't feel that you don't know who you are. Each time there is a problem in your life, you have a chance to drop an old view of yourself, but your energy goes into keeping the picture of who you are. You think that you are a 'continuous' person—but you are not. And if you would watch carefully, you would observe this. You are not some kind of a glued-together conglomerate of all those different views of yourself. You try to glue yourself together in the hope that you look nice to other people, especially the people you care about. When a part of you gets destroyed, when you are no longer a wife, for instance, what are you? There is an empty space and you fill it with "I am a rejected woman." I would suggest that when such a vacancy occurs in the picture of yourself, instead of filling it with another mentalization of 'who' you are, you hold part of you in a state of what I would call 'not knowing.' One part of you will acknowledge that you don't know who you are. The more of these moments you can develop, the more you will be in a state of not knowing. Observing these outer manifestations is important.

When you begin to meditate, you give yourself an opportunity to see the different parts of youself rise and fall all the time. One moment you see yourself one way, the next moment another; and if you are paying attention, you will observe a number of people, who are all you. You have a lot of views of yourself, and instead of seeing them all as continuing until you die, you begin to realize that they can be changed. You will not, in the beginning of your observations, let go of the views of yourself that you like—only the ones you don't like. So start where you are, and if you have a view of yourself that you do not like, I ask you with all sincerity to change it. You created it and *you can change it*. You don't have to go through life with a great crowd of people inside you because you really are not any of them anyway.

In meditation, as the physical body becomes more and more quiet, you will start to bring into your auric field other types of energy. The minute these other types of energy impinge on your physical frame, you will have various kinds of experiences. One kind of meditative experience is visions. There are two kinds of visions; those that make you feel happy and those that make you afraid. Behind every vision, whether beatific or demonic, there is something that is trying to catch your attention. Usually it is some view of yourself that you are trying to bring to your conscious mind so that you can drop it. For example, when you have a negative dream or vision that has a frightening or nightmarish quality about it, fear comes pouring in upon you. These are 'subconscious nightmares' that need to be brought into consciousness. When this is the case, whether it be visual or in a dream state, most of you run away. I would ask that you do not run from these visions. Part of your process is to bring this fear to your conscious recognition and the more you look upon it, the more helpful it becomes to you. There is no such thing as an 'evil' vision, dream or nightmare. If you have repeated dreams that are frightening, be aware that it is your Vast Self trying to bring unresolved patterns to your attention. You have already lived through your nightmares. You have seen them and you have come out the other end. They are not something that you have to continue to fear and to run from.

Your body will begin to respond to meditation and you may experience things like ringing in your ears, jerking of the body, or so much energy you feel like you've been plugged into a light

141

socket. You are likely to think that you are in physical danger and should quit. But I suggest, that instead of pulling away, you take it as a sign that the energy is at long last beginning to merge in some kind of intimate way with your body form. Just let it happen! So what if you have ringing in your ears; is that so much different from the modern music you play? Or what if your eyes begin to see things differently, or the physical world becomes a little fuzzy with edges a little wider? You might try this. Stare at the face of someone close to you, between the eyes and above, a soft kind of stare. You will find that everything begins to move. Your visual field will change and the face will start to change. It will become gorgeous or grisly, male or female, young or old. Any number of faces will appear and disappear.

It is a fact that when you put this kind of awareness on someone else and hold it steady, you will take the 'third eye' energy and blend yours with theirs. Other kinds of experiences will result. Then instead of wondering what your connection was in some past life, you will know that you are tuning in to some beautiful aspect of this one. Those of you who have been together for a long time have a more concrete vision of each other, for you have had more years in which to build it. It can be broken down. When you begin to work with this energy, you will see the 'otherness' of the person. You will begin to feel what it is that stands behind your rigid view of face and form. You will get feelings of greater vastness and begin to understand what it means when it is said that you are a mystery, that others are a mystery and there is something mysterious going on between you all the time.

What is the difference between a bonafide mental difficulty, and one that is a spiritually provoked, or energy provoked awareness? If after you have had one, you find that during the experience itself there was a feeling of energy, of upliftment, of interest, of desire to know more, then you may know that everything is on the right track. If, on the other hand, there is an *overwhelming* amount of fear, a feeling of total disorientation, or a feeling that one cannot get back, then perhaps you should not do deep meditation. But please be aware that if you are really on the Path, you will eventually come across some kind of experience that will not meet the common standards. And after all, that is what it is all about. If it were not, then why bother to go through all this? If you want your world to stay the same, to look, smell, and feel the same, why are you all here? You are looking for something extraordinary—but when it comes, fear also comes. Because the world tells you if you do not experience things in a continuous state, then you are unbalanced. I would tell you that I think you are 'unbalanced' if you *do* see things in a continuous way. If you are really looking, you will see that at one moment you are happy, in the next angry, in the next guilty, in the next sensual, in the next hungry, in the next sleepy. And can you tell me it is all the same? Can you really look at this incredible world of change, happy and sad, up and down, fear and joy, and see it as the same?

Why not try something a little different? Take the heretical position that you are none of these things. That what you are is the observer of an incredible variety of feelings, thoughts, and emotions. On the screen of who you are, let all of these things come and all of these things go. When fear is present, then fear is present; when joy is present, joy is present; anger, anger. If you can stop getting messed up in the machinery, you will find a great deal of freedom, for you are *not any one of those faces*. You think your biggest job is to keep yourself glued together. And when you have glued together all of these composite pictures of yourself and one of the elements falls out, or one turns against you, then what happens? That whole view of yourself becomes your enemy, somehow impinging on you. If you can only understand that you have defined yourselves in a certain way and that you can stop defining yourself in that way, you can start to be free.

When you go home tonight, I would ask you to list the ways in which you have defined yourself. Write down on a sheet of paper who you think you are. You will see a multifaceted entity that you

143

call 'yourself,' and you will see as you look at your list that you feel a need to maintain those faces to maintain a perfect view of yourself. Let us say that you have had a divorce. Your view of yourself then would be that you are a 'failure,' and you will realize that the view of yourself as married is now turning against you. Now let us say that you have a job, and you are fired. You will still feel a failure. What is attacking you is not your fear over not being able to pay your bills but your view of yourself as a successful and dynamic person. You feel vulnerable. When a part of you is taken away, such as a job, it is not the money that matters most. You can always make do with less, always. Why then do you feel so badly? Because a view of yourself as a successful person has now been replaced by a view of yourself as an unsuccessful person. If you can finally observe that these views of yourself, whether good or bad, are nothing more than stick-figures wandering through your life, having great fun doing what they want, then when one of them changes you will not feel so vulnerable. It is interesting to see that if you are successful in 99% of your undertakings and 1% unsuccessful, you will condemn yourself in your totality. And you will go around despondent, unhappy and frightened. Others will not see your life that way. They will see the many wonderful things that have happened. But you will bring out all of the negative stick-figures, and lay them out for others to see what a failure you are.

When you have set up the game so that you must be totally successful in your life, you are going to fail. You cannot be totally successful because you will win some and lose some and that is the way life goes. If you have the belief that every step you take has to be golden and wonderful, righteous and pure, you will fail. And it will not be in the external world that you will fail but in the internal world. You will become anxious anytime one of those stick-figures begins to get a little out of line and when you do, watch your pattern. First you will have to ignore all the good parts of your life. It is when you get into the pattern of paying attention to the part of you that is not going well, that—guess what, you have a failure. If you look long enough at your negative self, you will have the product for which you seek. If you can only understand that the way out of all of this is to simply stand back and watch your mind create infinite varieties of yourself, over and over again, you will see through the game.

You create with your mind. And when you understand that it is you who is doing the creating, two things happen. One, you free yourself from the tyranny of certain views of yourself; and two, you see that you have choices. Many of you are living lives under a tyranny that you have imposed upon yourselves; that tyranny comes from your refusal to see that any kind of negative experience you have is only one of myriads of events in your life. By your own choice, you return again and again to the negative events and they grow and get larger. The extent to which any event controls your life depends on the amount of energy you put into it. For example: people are standing on a street corner, a bus goes by and splashes mud on both of them. They should have the same response, for both have experienced the same event. Do you really think it will be so? One will forget it, but the other will spend days talking to his friends about the bus driver who spattered him with mud and how furious he is about it. The same event, the response different. Most of you who are tyrannized by a view of yourself are doing what the angry person is doing. You are revving up your motor so that you 'get behind' your negative view of yourself. But you have created, from one drop, a pitcher full of poison and you are the one who is drinking it. In the instant that the 'mud' descends, choice is present and you can drop the negative factor in yourself or you can enlarge it.

If you understand through meditation that what I am saying is real and not just talk, you can begin to be free. But you will never be free until you see that you have choices. When you get into any kind of deep meditation, you understand clearly that things come and things go. You can hang on or you can let go. *You create yourself, moment by moment, out of the responses in your mind.* People tell you that you create your own universe, your own reality. What does this mean? It means that out of the millions of thought forms that move through your mind, you choose the ones you will hang on to. You walk down the street. Three people will smile, two will frown. To whom will you pay attention? You wear some outrageous costume. Some think it terrific, others think you're nuts. To whom will you pay attention?

You choose and then build a picture of yourself and create your own universe day by day, thought by thought, choice by choice. It does not matter what is going on in your world. *You* select what you think about that world, and well you know it. Some people can lose their job and not be disturbed, while others will take a gun and commit suicide. I ask you to be very serious about this most basic step toward your own freedom. You can free yourself from tyranny without any trouble, if you will only see that it is you who selects and interprets and creates the picture of yourself day after day. If you don't like the picture *why not change it*? You change your view of yourself all the time. The problem is you do it unconsciously. In part, awakening involves the realization that you create your view of yourself and the events of your life. Once you understand that, you are in a position of power. If you don't want to be resentful then make another choice. If you do want to be resentful, then choose it. It doesn't matter what you choose, but that *you choose*.

This may be spiritual heresy, but sometimes it is just plain fun to get angry! If you *choose* anger, it can be exciting and not necessarily destructive. But if you unconsciously move toward anger and an explosion comes, you will be filled with guilt, remorse and resentment, because half of you wants to be angry and the other half refuses to acknowledge it. So, if you are good at swallowing your anger and smile instead, then your view of yourself as a 'loving person' has not changed. It gives you a lot of mileage. Understand that you do this daily. There is a difference between 'clean' anger and 'dirty' anger. Clean anger comes from making specific statements and taking full responsibility. Dirty anger makes the other person responsible and throws all of their 'faults' at them.

You are in the seat of control all the time, but you are not conscious of it. 'Awakening' means that you are awake and aware of all the possible thought forms and know you do have a choice. So, instead of choosing those that make you miserable, perhaps you might be wise enough to choose others. You don't eat the same meal all the time and if something is distasteful to you, you move on to something more pleasant.

But, you don't do the same with regard to emotional responses that are distasteful to you. You see your girlfriend talking to another boy and you are sick. But there are other responses, other choices. There is no great God who says that you must be angry, or jealous or self-pitying. You have abdicated the power of your own control, and I ask you to re-establish yourself in the center of your own choices. And the easiest, the fastest and most exciting way to do that is to *pay attention to what your mind is thinking*. See the faces that come and the faces that go. Some of your choices were made years ago, when you were about two feet tall. You saw the world as a frightening place to live and you continue to respond to that fear. Now you are six feet two, in charge of a great corporation and totally powerful. Yet, if someone comes up to you and says something negative, you again become a frightened little child. It is not necessary. The choices you made then need not be the choices you make now. If you could only understand that, literally, you create your own world, you would become excited about your own possibilities. But they will never come into form until you yourself have decided to see them.

You think it is very hard to make other choices. But it is possible! You see your boyfriend talking to a girl that is much more gorgeous than you. You know all the negative choices, so think about some of the positive ones, for they are there also. And out of the vast repertoire of infinite possibilities, you can choose another one. You refuse to make another choice because you still believe you can change the other person. You still think if you go to your boyfriend and demand that he not talk to that gorgeous girl because it makes you feel terrible, he will do as you ask. Maybe he will and if he does you will think that you have won. But you have given up your power by abdicating your responsibility. You have not had to do anything but ask him to change. As long as you are addicted to the idea that manipulating your universe from the outside will make you happy, you will not change. It is this type of manipulation that in the end will imprison you both. Now he has the right to tell you not to do something he does not like. And you will be obligatd to do it, for you have made a trade-off. You make trade-offs all the time in your relationships. In the end you will see that you are limiting each other day after day and are both equally imprisoned. If you learn only one thing in this lifetime, let it be this: *you are responsible for your own happiness.* And you accomplish this by changing your responses to the events that happen in your life.

The more you meditate, the more you practice self-awareness, and the more you experience moment-to-moment living; the more the power that brings about all physical, mental, and visual transformations will start to aid you. Having more of that kind of power around you, you will feel more secure in your ability to make changes. And this is why I say over and over, please, if you love yourself, find some way to practice centered awareness because out of that centered awareness you will build a power-base that you can count on in times of extremity. You will have a bank account to draw upon when things get rough and you want to make another choice. A 'weak person' is in no position to control his own life. So build your power, build your centeredness, build a feeling of rapport with your own inner Self. Build that feeling of power within yourself and you *can* make changes, you *can* make choices, you *can* select differently. As your body and your mind begin to change, things happen. You are not a block of concrete. You are a wonderful conglomeration of moving energy fields. And as these shift and change, your whole outlook changes and the mystery of life begins to unfold. It all starts with sitting down and shutting up! And listening and feeling and allowing and experiencing—that's all it takes. One of the greatest obstacles to your happiness is the belief that your world makes you miserable. It is *your response to your world* that makes you miserable. Please understand that as deeply as you can. Put yourself in control. People trip you up because they want you to feel guilty because when you feel guilty enough, you will do what they want you to do. The sad feature is that changing another's behavior is never enough, because it is not the other who is the source of your happiness.

Q: Do enlightened people make conscious choices?

The totally enlightened one makes no choices because he sees no difference in one course over another and has absolutely no preference. The enlightened one knows that they, the choice, and every event are one and he does not care what side or position he is on. So at that stage it is a choiceless life.

But prior to that, there is another state. It is not necessary that you reach total enlightenment on the earth plane. There is another state which many of you can reach, and which I would like to discuss. When you finally learn that you do have choices, the first step is to make choices that better your own life, your own perceptions, your own inner relationship with your universe. And I applaud that, for you will develop more inner power. The next stage is to make choices that benefit others first. This is the realm of the true spiritual Teacher, who takes on the 'karma' or the 'illness' of the student. This is an area of service that you get into when you willingly make your choices on behalf of others, even knowing that in so doing you may suffer.

To make that choice for others from the ego would indeed be slavery for many but made from the Self, when fully conscious of the results, those choices are true surrender. And that is a space from which many of you can operate. I will not pretend that you can reach the state of an Avatar but you can, once you understand that you hold choices and begin to choose for yourself. Then will come a day when you will choose for others. And what about you?

In the realm of the surrendered one comes a feeling of peace truly beyond description. It comes not because you are so 'holy' but because you know that in the next instant the choice could be made for yourself; but you don't care anymore. Many of you are capable of that, and I present it as an inspiration. Then you have the true world servers, the ones who do not serve because it makes them feel good, but simply because they saw a choice and out of their being comes the response they want to make, they make it and it's done. I repeat, many of you are capable of that kind of response and I would ask you to give due thought to moving toward it. It would be well received.

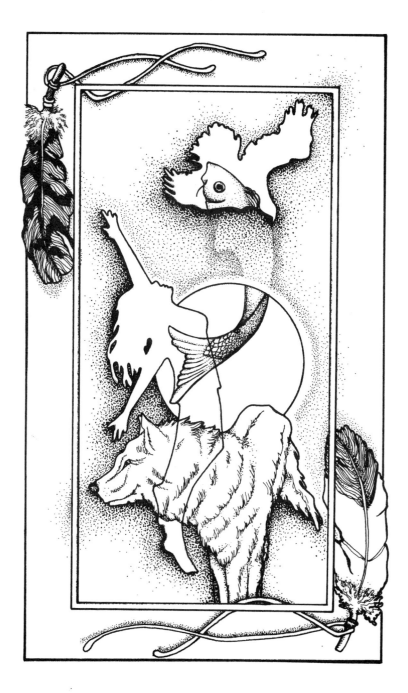

THE MESSAGE OF ST. FRANCIS
19 December 1982
Albuquerque, New Mexico

This is the time for the celebration of the coming of the Christ to the earth plane. But instead of speaking of the Christos today, I would like to bring forward another figure who is termed a 'Christian,' because I feel that he may better exemplify your own dilemma. Now who, and why?

I would like to speak of the one whom you have come to call St. Francis of Assisi. The reason for that selection, rather than the Christ, is because we have been working in the past months on the idea that our beliefs bring about our reality. In the case of the Christos, or the Christ as you would call him, there was very little need for him to change or modify his belief structure. He came from a plane of understanding where those modifications had taken place long before. Whatever obstacles he had left were so minor that I do not feel that they would make a good comparison with yours. That entity was of such stature that 'ground work' was not needed. But in the case of St. Francis, we have a different situation. He can stand as a tremendous hope for many people.

We have been working at length toward the understanding that the power of the Vastness moves constantly through you and out into the world, creating the world as you see it. Before that power becomes form and matter, it moves through a structure or 'gridwork,' which is the belief system through which you create your world. When we speak of St. Francis, we are speaking about a man who was, in truth, very similar to many of you. He had unfinished business in the world; pools of desire, anger, lust, of all the things for which you so condemn yourselves. He also contained, just as you do, infinite possibilities to become the person that he did. I do not mean that you all should try to become 'St. Francis,' but I do mean that there lies within you the same possibilities for changing your belief structure so that you can come into contact with the knowledge of God's existence. This is the issue. The only difference between Francis and yourselves is that he came to know that God was and he knew, that he could be in touch with that reality at any time. *He knew it*, with all the power of his being. That potential you also have, and so you share a similarity with him.

Francis had, as a youth, the same lusts that you have, the same avarice, the same desires for popularity, for drink, for women, for fun, for excitement, for power. And when he became aware that these activities were not giving him the joy that he had thought they would, he became even more of what he had been. He began to drink more, to 'sin' more, to carry all of his desires to the extreme. But out of the overindulgence of his so-called 'sinful' side, he became very aware of the obstacles that his human consciousness had to overcome.

His reasoning was somewhat thus: "It is impossible for me to be a 'good' person, for I have all of these imperfections, so I will become the 'perfect sinner'! I will expand the areas of all of my deficiencies to vaster degrees, and perhaps out of that 'perfection' I will find some kind of joy and harmony in my life." But in the end, he found that this also did not give him that which he wanted, and so a dilemma arose in his mind. I hope that the same dilemma arises in yours. You cannot always be loving or kind, and indulging your desires has not brought happiness—so where can you go to find the inner peace and joy you seek? Francis chose a very meaningful way. Again, I do not recommend it; I only present is as an example.

Francis decided (and I state this with assurance) at a very deep level, to confront the reality of death. He chose a strong and powerful illness, and when he became ill almost unto death, the boundaries in his mind began to fall and in the heat of his fever, he came to an understanding. He saw that he had tried to equate 'goodness' with 'love of God,' and they were not at all the same. You can love God, without being 'good.' And you can be very 'good,' and have no love of God! Francis realized clearly that his love of God was determined by *his desire to love God*. It was a tremendously important moment when he saw the fallacy of his belief. *You love God through loving God*, and not from anything else. Then, in the midst of his fever the question came, over and over: *How* can I love God? How? Remember that this man was brought up in the Church, also in a society which was only superficially religious. And his friends certainly were not deeply religious. His mother represented the need to love God, but not the manifestation of the love of God.

Francis felt that if he could not find a way to love God, then his wish was to die. He could not live without loving God—but he didn't know how! I would suggest that this is a very fortunate state to be in; to see clearly the paradox of *wanting* to love, but not knowing how.

Day after day the struggle went on. The fever increased, the anxiety increased, and the frustration and the hopelessness increased. Finally, early one morning as the dawn began to break, when all was very quiet and still, Francis heard a bird outside his window— but he heard it in a totally new way. In the power of the song of that bird, he understood! And what he understood was the way to love God and the *only* way was to hear his voice in *everything*; in the song of a bird, in the cry of the dying, in the scream of the mad, in the despair of the leper, in the embrace of the lovers—*that was the way to love God!* He knew, absolutely, that there was no separation between those sounds and the 'Voice of God'—that they *are* the Voice of God. He had been mistaken in placing God outside of the created world, outside of the sounds of life, outside of himself! Never again in his life did he fail to remember that. If we speak of Francis as 'enlightened,' his 'enlightenment' would come from the fact that he was so very ordinary—and out of that became so totally extra-ordinary. From that moment on, he could never again

155

separate out any call for help from the Source he now knew to be real.

There have been some misconceptions about Francis, and one of them concerns his relationship with his father. It has been said that there was much hostility between Francis and his father. But since in his new awareness, he knew that every sound was God speaking, it was not possible for him to reject the sound of his father's voice when his father told him to leave his house. Francis said, "Yes father, I hear you. Thank you for showing me my next step." It was not, "How dare you?"—but "I hear you." And so he went.

When he began his life alone, and heard the voice command, "Rebuild my church!" he knew that it spoke to more than one level. But when he heard the words, the only obvious thing to do was to rebuild a physical church, and trust that in the building of it, something else would come—the building of another 'church,' on another level. Francis did not consult anyone, nor did he ask the Pope for permission, he decided to do what was before him. I would ask you to think about that for your own lives. If you wish to know what God wants of you, ask and *you will know*. And when you do, please do not wait, but act today on what you know now! There is not one of you who cannot begin today, to build, or to rebuild, some kind of 'church.' There is no one who does not have some part of them that is in need of 'repair.' Do not wait until you can do something more spectacular, instead of doing that which is before you. Please, the lesson is simple. If you have something to rebuild, start there, no matter how unglamorous it may seem, no matter how mundane or how difficult. And if you want to know what your 'unfinished church' is, just *ask*!

So Francis leaves his home, and he goes alone, with the knowledge that there is no longer any of the separation which had kept him so confused. He seems strange to many because of the one great realization that *God is in everything*. He goes about talking of 'Brother Wind, Brother Sky'; he talks to birds, to animals, to insects, to everything. He appears to many as a lunatic, but when you understand his new basic belief, you can understand why he chose to personify it in the way that he did. When the wind blew, when he felt the sun, he *knew* that it was God caressing him; he *knew that* it was God's breath upon him, he *knew* that the rain and the mud were the God of his Being! And when he heard the chattering of the animals, he *knew* he was hearing the One Voice, and there was no separation, nor could there ever be. He embraced the leper, not because he was courageous, but because he saw no difference between them!

Francis is not 'courageous'; there is no 'Francis' left to be courageous, just God meeting God, in all the many aspects of life. People thought him very humble when he told them it was not hard. It is not hard to be cold, when you know that the cold is God. It is not hard to be struck by a stone when you know that the stone is God. For the rest of his life, he moved with this deepest understanding that *nothing is separate*. And people would remark how courageous it was of Francis not to be afraid of death, or of starvation. His response was, "How can there be fear of death, when death and I are one?" People thought him very exalted and very holy, to be so humble. But he denied it all. He did not see himself as holy nor humble; he perceived himself as *everything* and at the same time, as *nothing*.

So moving beyond this early times, we come to a subject I would most like to talk about, which is of course, the stig,mata. *Your belief creates your reality*. Francis spent many moments of his life praying for one thing only—to be able to share, totally, in the life of his Beloved—and his beloved was the crucified Christ. Inside himself he knew that his life would not be complete until he too, had suffered like that. He knew that the stigmata would be not only physically painful, but also very difficult to carry in a world of such tremendous confusion. Nonetheless, every day he prayed, "Let me share that, too!" Be aware that had he prayed for something different, the stigmata would not have come to him. It was his

157

yearning for the stigmata, not as an outward sign of his 'holiness,' but as the final blending of his heart with that of the Christ that he prayed for. Had he yearned for something other, that is what would have manifested. That which you put your awareness upon, you get! If Francis stands for anything, he demonstrates the power of mind over matter. He stands as an example of the power of belief over the material world. Think about it. Here is a man with an ordinary body, no different from yours, but one day, upon a mountain, in response to days and nights of prayer and fasting and crying and waiting, there appears what you have now called the 'stigmata.' It is Energy moving from the Vastness onto the mountain, and as it approaches, he knows without question that when the Light enters him, he will never again be the same. And he has no way of knowing what the results will be. He might go insane, or be blinded, or deafened, or seared so badly that he will never move again. He *knows* the chance he is taking. In the last, as that Power came, there was a communication, and a Voice asked, "Will you enter totally into my heart?" and he answers, *"I will!"* Remember, he knows, that in an instant everything can be utterly transformed—into darkness and pain, or into Light and Freedom. And he says, "Yes, take me! I cannot live without You! Do with me as you will!"

And it is at this point that Francis demonstrates his courage, not before. This is *real* courage, because Francis is the only one who knows the power of this Energy! For years, he had been experiencing that Energy, slowly at first, but always gathering momentum, and now when he sees this vortex of Power, he knows, that it can do anything. The power enters, and the marks are made.

God does not move without purpose; so why did He ask this beloved one (and he was beloved—as are you) to carry these bleeding wounds with him for the rest of his days? They were very painful wounds, especially in the unsanitary world of his time. So, why? It is the same symbol, then and now. You believe that you are the body, and that the body has a life of its own; and you do not believe in the power of spiritual thought. Francis would tell you that what you dwell upon, *you will receive*! So if he had the power to call to him the signs of the stigmata, is it not possible that *you* have the power, within you, to call to you the Light for which you are looking? If he was able to transform even the dense matter of his cellular structure, can you not also *create your reality!* One of the most powerful forces that you have is your mind. And this is what I would ask you to hear from Francis.

It is not necessary for you to duplicate the externals of his life, but it is important that you understand the amazing power that you have, and are not using. Please dwell upon what happened to this man. One ordinary man, with one extraordinary desire! You too have an extraordinary desire—and whatever that desire is, is what is now manifesting in your life! If you wish to know God, then Francis is a most helpful example for you. You *can* follow his way, for it is the inner way. What he did on the outside is not important, what he did on the inside is infinitely important. And that, you can also do. If you wish to know God you can—but you will have to make it an extraordinary desire! One way is to know that every moment you are speaking, you are not speaking to others, you are speaking to God. Is this required of you? If you wish to know God in the way that Francis did, then perhaps so.

Remember what it was that Francis learned from the song of the bird: God's voice speaks through everyone and everything—and that included the townspeople. They were upset because their finest sons were following this 'ruffian.' Francis was not a glamorous man. In fact, there are many homes today where he would not be welcome at the back door, let alone the front! He probably smelled badly and he didn't speak rationally; and when he did speak, the townspeople could not understand him. It is hard to understand someone who said that God is speaking in the birds or talking through the wind. And when their sons, upon whom they had placed all their future hopes, go to follow this strange man, to laugh, to pray, to sing, to talk, what are they to do? However much

Francis is loved now, they certainly did not love him then! People saw him as a danger to their lives; and something that has not been sufficiently recorded is the threat of physical danger to Francis, with angry families coming to repossess their children. "This lunatic Francis has been out in the sun too long. Put some money on your head, my son, it will cool you off! Come home!" Francis realized the danger of his position, and decided to lay the problem before the Pope. His concern was for the safety of his brothers.

Francis travels to see the Pope. There has been much nonsense written about this phase, but one thing did happen. Before Francis entered what is now known as the Vatican, the Pope did begin to have strange dreams, and strange feelings about a person who turned out to be Francis. Why? Since Francis was not separate from the Pope, and he was on his way to speak to the Father, like all good Fathers, the Pope knew that his son was coming. However negative you might feel about those Popes, the fact remains that they had some degree of true spiritual understanding, and one of the main understandings of that time was of the 'power of the vision.' In those days, dreams and visions were sought and respected. And so the Pope and those around him listened to those visions and the message was clear: someone is coming with a request; you aren't going to like it, but please, pay attention. No more than that, but that was enough. Understand that there was no way in the world that Francis could have approached the Pope, had not others allowed him. Whatever your fantasies may be, you do not just walk in the door, ask to see the Pope, and get ushered into his presence. Especially in those days.

When Francis came, the Pope understood something. He had the power of observation, not only of the physical, but the ability to observe energy. The Popes in those days prayed, and they prayed a lot. They prayed a lot more than they do now, for they had less work, less 'red tape,' and one of the ways of observation is through prayer. This Pope was not a fool. Please do not make these people into stereotypes. This was an amazingly prayerful man, and he did not carry the weight of his office lightly. When he was in the presence of Francis and his followers, he felt something; and what he felt was their power, and he understood that Francis was the man of his visions. And no, he did not like it. The petition to become a true Order is presented for his approval. Inwardly, the Pope is afraid, because the powers around his throne are against this. And this is where he becomes courageous. He says, "I will do it. I will make you a real arm of God! I *will* do it!"

The most important part of this decision is not the building of the Franciscan Order. It is because, from that moment on, Francis did not have to worry about his brothers, for he knew they were safe. Now he is free to totally immerse himself in his inner prayer. His concern was never for himself, but for what they would have had to undergo. He is ready to begin the walk that ended on the mountain.

What then, does all this have to do with you? Perhaps to ask you to look deeply at those things that are causing you anguish, and realize that they stand as the barrier to your walk up your mountain to Freedom. Once you know and recognize the areas that produce your anxieties, and once you see that the time you spend agonizing over these matters does not help you, you may be moved to put those affairs in order, to resolve them and silence them. Until you do that, the part of your mind that is in anguish will continue to move in anguish, and you will not be whole-hearted.

Let us join Francis again as he moves through the last phase of his life. The stigmata is embarrassing to him, but he cannot hide it. He does his best to keep it to himself, but the news travels fast, and soon everyone knows; so wherever he goes, even to the smallest villages, people come—not to hear him talk about God, but to touch the stigmata. And in being drawn to the stigmata, they listen to the man. At this stage of his life, he is not well—but he does not care, for health and illness are the same. But, day after day, the crowds grab the bleeding wounds.

The choice to withdraw, to isolate himself, to hide from the lay people of his world, to care for himself, to make things easier, was a constant temptation directed at him by the pleadings of his brothers. His answer was always the same: "God did not give this to me for myself alone! Either I share it with all, or it has no meaning." And so, if you will look carefully at your lives, you will see there is not one of you who has not been given a gift. Not one. If you choose to use your gift to keep yourself safe, secure, and comfortable, that is one choice. But every time you share your gift, whether it be nursing, therapy, teaching, painting, child-rearing, or whatever; every time you share it whole-heartedly, no matter how inconvenient, you *will* touch God. The gift was given to you so that it could be shared. Not only at your convenience, but because you know that when you share this gift, you live your life not for yourself, but for other people. Those of you who see no purpose in life, please look to this. Your life will not be worth anything until you learn to serve others. A life lived selfishly will never make you happy!

So the end comes; and while it may be true that the brothers sorrowed, I can assure you that Francis did not. And even in his death, there was something to learn. In his passing, the brothers wept, and they who had traveled for so long together beg Francis to stay. And he asked them why. "Because we love you! We love you! We will miss you!" And he replies, "You haven't learned very much, have you?" They are taken aback and ask him what he means. He replies, "I thought you knew. *It is all one!* The death and the life are all one! I thought you knew. If God be in the wind, is he not also in death? If all space be full, will you ever be empty? If you are a part of everything, how can anything ever be taken from you? How could anything *ever* be taken from you?" But they did not understand.

When he had gone, those few of the brothers that were closest to him began to understand; because as they sat under the trees and heard the wind, they remembered him, and knew that the sound of the wind was not separate from Francis. And they felt better. When they sat in the sun, and felt its warmth, they remembered his song, and they knew that the sun was not separate from Francis, and they felt better. When they cared for the sick, they knew that he was there, and they felt better. So perhaps in his dying, the deepest teaching was given—which is, *you can never be separated*, no matter what your eyes might tell you, or what your pain might say, you can never be separated from that which you love. So just love totally—and in loving, nothing can ever be taken from you again.

THE COMFORTER
15 December 1985
Albuquerque, New Mexico

It is our observation that the Season upon which you are entering presents both a delight and a dilemma. The delight is in the anticipation, and the dilemma is that the anticipation does not come to life. The anticipation is that on a certain day the Christ awareness will be born in you, so you look forward to it, move toward it and then, on the day that the birthing was to occur, nothing had changed. It is our hope today to give you a gift, a gift of remembering what was bestowed on you a long time ago. We ask that you remember this gift and then allow us to share with you ways in which you can, in the beauty and wonder of your own Beingness, manifest that gift so that you will know without question that you are not alone and the birth that you are looking for has already taken place.

In order to do this, I would like to read a message given to you thousands of years ago from an old friend of yours named Jesus. He was speaking at the time when He knew that He would be leaving the physical plane and, because of His great love, wanted to leave something behind. He is speaking to His close friends:

"And I will pray to the Father and He shall give you another Comforter, that He may abide with you forever. It is the Spirit of Truth Whom the world cannot receive because it sees Him not, neither can it know Him. But you will know Him, for He dwelleth with you and shall be in you. I will not leave you comfortless. But the Comforter, which is the Holy Ghost, whom the Father will send in My Name, He shall teach you all things and bring all things to your remembrance . Let not your heart be troubled, neither let it be afraid, for I am with you always."

It seems to me that you have two choices around this kind of a statement. Either you choose to believe that whoever spoke it was at the height of his arrogant power and knew not what he said, or he in some way had an intimate relationship with that energy which he calls Father. And that he knew that there was to be an exchange made and in the exchange, something enduring, something everlasting and something totally reachable was going to be left for mankind. The Comforter has been with you ever since. Perhaps the difficulty is that you have become confused between two things: the feeling of the Comforter on one hand and on the other hand, the pain, anguish and dilemmas of your daily life. Many people have asked the simple question, "What are we here for?" There are many ways to answer that. I would like to present one of them for your consideration that fits in deeply with the image of the Comforter.

Every time one of you suffers a personal disaster such as the loss of a child through death and moves victoriously out of the abyss, you have provided this earth plane with a greater standard of courage than it had before. Every time one of you endures tremendous physical pain with dignity and humor you have contributed to the overall power and wonder of this planet. Every time you have had the choice of anger and have instead selected understanding, you have added to the sum total of the available power, courage and wisdom that this planet runs on. *Every day of your life you live for the purpose of generating some kind of power* and that power is not something small. It extends far past your own lives and goes out into the planetary system and gives other entities courage when they need it. It gives the entire race a vaster sense of who they are. Your job, in one way of speaking, is to empower the human race in every possible way that you can. The victories that you have every day, as small as they might be and as vast as they might be, are why you are here. You are not here to obtain some mysterious standard of perfection. Every day you have a chance of participating with your purpose in wonder and power and awareness, and in so doing increase the vibrational frequency of the entire earth experience, now and on into the future. Your lives have a daily purpose, and it is nothing vast and miraculous like angels dancing in your living rooms. What it has to do with is the knowledge that you are a power generator and in so generating you make a difference. The difficult part comes when the difference you make does not meet your own standards. There are those moments of your sorrow when you know that you cannot speak truth or you cannot overcome your self-pity because of some fear that is within you. Somehow this moment of this day, you just don't have the necessary opening to be able to come up to your own high standards. It is at this juncture that I would ask you to deeply consider the gift that we have just discussed.

For many of you, the Comforter is an intellectual exercise. You hear the words and you go about your business. The Comforter has a lot of trouble reaching those of you who do that, my friends. The Comforter, in my terms, is an incredibly vast energy source that has an electromagnetic connection with your own energy field. Within the physical apparatus that you call the body, you have an electromagnetic magnet, cellularly present, that connects up with the electromagnetic field of what we will call the Power of the Comforter. The thing that triggers this field *is your choosing of it*. You can sit in a room with a television set that is perfectly operable and unless you turn it on, nothing happens. Nor do you expect anything to happen because you clearly understand your responsibility in relationship to that event. So I ask you to use all of that beautiful wisdom around your television set and transpose it to a vaster realm and say clearly, "I hold myself responsible for the flipping on of this wonderful current." Many of you do this and I am grateful. I am grateful because I want you to be happy, but just as important I am grateful because every time that you do this you end up helping people far past your range of vision. You ask to be world servers but that has a connotation in your mind that ends up being something very fancy. The kind of world server I am talking about is the one who, every day of his life makes the conscious choice of flipping that switch, keeping the magnetic current alive, knowing that when you remember what the Comforter means, the connection is made, and in so doing, the energy fields around you begin to take on a different power. Your life will then change from the inside, not the outside.

Some of you are suffering from tremendous boredom. Boredom is easily overcome by increased power, increased energy. Most of the time you do this by going out into the world and changing your energy relationships—new jobs, new lovers, new cars, whatever. And that's fine. But that can be expensive and so I would suggest a device that is a little closer to home. What you really want when you are bored is to feel life in a new way, to feel dynamic awareness, power and extension—to feel alive. You want to feel life moving in you so strongly that just feeling it, no matter what you are doing, is enough on its own. And that's what it means to 'turn on' the remembrance of the Comforter. I know in the beginning it is difficult, when nothing happens, you quickly get discouraged and you do not ever make the connection. Teachers such as the Christ agree on one thing, *stick with it and you will feel the Comforter*. You will not think it, you will feel it and you will know it. The Comforter will begin to move and have its being in you. And those choices always rest with you. To come out of another frame of consciousness and force itself into your electromagnetic field is an invasion of your privacy and cannot be done.

So, if we could talk about the Comforter in energy terms and not as some kind of stereotypical form, we will be able to bypass your preconceptions about it. The minute we say 'form' we are in trouble. All of you have form and the one thing you know about form is that sometimes it likes you and sometimes it doesn't. Sometimes you please it and sometimes you displease it. Sometimes it loves you and sometimes it leaves you. Form is unpredictable in your lives. When you think of 'form,' a pattern of resistance is set up in you. This is not a conscious thing. Coming up out of your awareness is the remembrance of all of the times that form has disappointed you. Again and yet again it disappoints you, so you put up barriers. So when I ask you to dwell on the Comforter, please, no form, just Knowing. Just as you watch the clouds moving across your mesas, knowing that something moves them but you know not what, spend that time watching motion, knowing that motion is present, moving things and breaking them up. Look at the naturalness of your world, it speaks to you as one of the most direct mirrors of your awareness.

You have come a long way from feeling natural in your natural world and one of the things that most ignites the soul is to see and feel your relationship to the naturalness of all that is around you. What does it mean to see the sun rising every day? There are deep allegorical meanings that come alive in your psyche when you see the clouds and feel the power that moves them, when you feel the wind taking you and pushing you into some new kind of formation. These events speak to places inside of you that the mind cannot reach. Some of you go on holiday and really think that it is the martinis and the skiing that delights you. The delight comes because you and the wind are there and the snow is there and the naturalness is there, and all of those inner symbols that you have carried with you since you began your earth journey are ignited. In your embracing of that moment *you feel the Power, the Love, the Life of that which you call the Divine.* These are natural symbols that live within you and when you are in relationship to those remem-brances, you become empowered. Not because you sit in the sun on the beach and get a glorious tan, but because in that delight of feeling the sand beneath you, of hearing the waves and feeling the wonder of the sun, you remember your connection to them all. You have become very sophisticated, and one of the difficulties with being sophisticated is a negation of the natural. My friends, they do not have to be separate. There can be a wondrous marriage between the two. And I ask you to remember this, if on Christmas afternoon you feel depressed, rise up, go out, and start to feel what life is all about. Open yourself and listen and smell and feel, and become alive and participate and share and give. Ignite the symbols inside of you that let you know you have a purpose, that let you know *there is a God and you are alright.* The kind of awareness gained by the stimulation of remembering the symbols inside of you can change your life. But to simply sit there in front of the television will not do the same thing—even if your team wins.

So, the Comforter can be smelled, heard, felt and experienced when you move out of your isolation and into the openness of things. There isn't anything you need to do except to open and allow yourself to feel. It is difficult to feel when you are constricted with pain. But when you are out in the vastness of things, you will be safe enough to allow yourself to feel. Pick your places and do it with care, the care that says you love yourself enough to make sure that you are safe before you open up your being. And when you do, know that the feeling that starts moving through you is the Comforter. It is an energy vortex that will come the minute that you express the desire to feel it. That desire triggers the mechanism that joins you, by your remembrance. Turn your mind to the Comforter when you feel lonely or anxious and need something to fill and uplift you. That is when you make that electromagnetic connection.

The necessity to understand that you are the trigger that connects you with worlds that are not physical is the beginning of your freedom from pain and suffering and sorrow. You are not kept alive by the physical senses, yet the data of those senses is what you think you live by. I beg you to take a new view, even for a little while, and to see that there might be some truth in the statement that you are a spherical state of awareness, beautifully, wonderfully empowered, that has *never left* the point of Source from which all this came. You have never left that point of interface where you and Source chose to rise up and manifest as human consciousness. It interfaces with you constantly. It is not lost, nor is it hidden. That point simply needs activation through consciousness. And that means being responsible for turning your awareness deeply within yourself and choosing to feel the Comforter. You cannot create the Comforter, it is already there. Jesus says It will teach you all things.

That teaching happens all the time. It happens constantly within you and outside of you. The difficulty is that much of the time you are not listening on the right frequency. The wonderful thing is that you are not a television set, nor are you a radio. You are capable of receiving material from different frequencies and assimilating them in your physical body at the same time. In your amazing body which so many of you try to denigrate, is a mechanism for hearing and receiving and blending the material that comes in. You choose what you are going to experience just as clearly as you do when you go to select a book in a bookstore. You make the selection with consciousness. Make the same conscious inner selection moment by moment. When you are in the midst of a difficulty stop and say, "I would like to experience the incredible peace of the Comforter NOW." When you become afraid, quietly say, "I wish to experience the peace of the Comforter *now*." That desire is the trigger.

Many of you have chosen at some point in your lives to be alone. You either realize the wisdom of what you have done and choose to make maximum of it, or you spend a lot of time complaining about why it happened and how to get out of it. If it is in your destiny to have a deep and abiding relationship, the relationship will come. Even if you are seated in a monk's closet, someone will knock on the door and you will feel the necessity to answer and so the relationship will be. On the other hand, if the necessary lesson of this part of your lifetime is to discover how to generate, by yourself, in your own physical body the wondrous sense of nourishment, fulfillment and power that is possible, then it will be thus. *Trust* what happens to you, please. When you don't trust the power of your own lives, you feel that somehow it's a mischance, that something has gone wrong, that the mechanism has gone awry and someone has put a spanner in the works and you are stuck with a terrible life. But everything that happens to you happens, to you deeply according to your own blueprint pattern.

I have told you before that you are born with a very direct, vast and

171

open blueprint of how your destiny is going to unfold in any given lifetime. You know, if you are taking a trip to the Far East, you at least find out how to get there and you know where you want to go and you are smart enough to take a certain amount of equipment with you. Well, do you not think that when you come to the earth plane to this kind of experience that you would not have the same wisdom? Do you really feel that you have only earth plane wisdom? Is it not possible that that wisdom functions outside of time and space, outside of body form and that you would not choose to spend forty, fifty, eighty years here without any kind of predestination, or idea of where you are going, or what you are going to encounter? If you grant that you manifest logic here, does it not follow that, out of the limitations of body, in a vaster state of awareness, you would use that time to make your life selections for the benefit of the wholeness of not only yourself but of the planet, too? Nothing happens in the vast parts of your life by chance. I do not mean things like what kind of car will you buy, but the big powerful brush strokes of your life that were designed by you with expert grace, balance and harmony before you came. If *you* planned it, it's got to be useful, it's got to be able to empower you in whatever way is meaningful to your life. It's opening up to that possibility that allows the inner vision to come. Whatever seems meaningful, will open the inner vision because it gives you courage. *Inner vision will give you courage*, the courage to acknowledge the wisdom of your planning and the execution of whatever it is that you have planned. Your inner vision guides you as clearly as anything can. It is the surety of the total purposefulness of every day of your life. You become desperate and depressed because you have forgotten that every day of your life has a purpose. To any extent whatsoever that you practice any of the empowering truths such as love, humor, vision, acceptance, courage, discipline, wisdom you are building in yourself an empowered energy field that makes the next day easier to be courageous in. It sets up an electromagnetic current around you which gives the people around you an opportunity to become bolder and more courageous. Then they in turn go out and effect the lives of others.

172

When you choose this everything begins to change in your life. And it's an accumulated awareness.

The reason that the teachers have yelled different spiritual disciplines at you is not because there is anything particularly holy about any one of them, but because they are trying to trick you into remembering. Doesn't it strike you as odd that there are so many different paths? Well, is it not possible that underlying all of those differences there is the desire to help you trick yourself into remembering to flip the switch that allows the current to flow between you and that which you are seeking? That loving supportive energy has always been hovering around you. Even in your most despairing moments, as you are crying out, the thing that you are looking for surrounds you. But, instead, at those points everything goes into a holding pattern. The entire physical and emotional vehicle freezes. You hold very still, because you don't want to feel more pain than you think you can bear. When you say you become well, that the pain has left, it is because you begin to loosen up inside. All of the inner symbols that you have not been able to touch upon in that frozenness begin to come alive in the thaw, slowly, slowly. And they tell you on a deep level that you can trust this process. Then moment by moment, day by day, sometimes year by year, comes the reawakening of the trust. The symbols of trustworthiness for the entire process of life are deeply embedded within you. So those of you who have been or will go into deep stress, just remember it's as if you freeze and then you slowly, gently thaw and to whatever extent you can accept them, the symbols come alive. Those of you who are loving those people in times of stress, simply hold them in your warmth and in your caring and that will help the melting process. Words will do nothing. Energy is the only gift, the open gift. Give them your energy and allow them to use it for the thawing of their position. There is no one who, if their desire is strong enough, cannot move into a deep relationship with the Life that always surrounds them, and most specifically with the Comforter.

The reason that I ask you to think about the Comforter is because the Comforter has a job to do. That energy vortex has a purpose, a stated, specific purpose, just as you have stated specific purpose in your life. So when you call on the Comforter to do what It has come to do, the participation between you can be instantaneous. There is a way of connecting with this energy almost every conscious moment of your life. The people who achieve that are called enlightened and it is a nice term because you could say that they have turned on the light. The only difference between any of you and an enlightened one is that the enlightened one believed that it was true that there was a vortex of energy that could augment their life in a direct way. And they decided to take a chance. Nobody gets enlightened unless they take a chance. If you are waiting for proof, you are going to wait a long time. You simply have to take a chance. Take a risk.

What would happen if for one year you gave yourself the job of 'remembrance' as many moments of the day as you could? This is the kind of thing that delights the Divine—let's make it a challenge. What if I'm lying? Could be. I would love to have proof come into your life and that would happen if you decide to risk. You read the books to get the courage to risk. The difficulty is that some of you have read hundreds of books and when it comes time to take the risk you get confused because there are so many paths to the Light. I suggest you get very simple, settle down deeply in your psyche and acknowledge that you are ready to feel love and peace and power, ready to risk. The risk you take is great because what happens if nothing is there? What if it turns out that ego moving through ego response is all that there is, that ever has been, ever will be? The last risk is always this one—do you have the courage to take the chance that there really is nothing greater than what you experience now? There is absolutely no question that in reality there is a power that you call the Divine that comes to you, that teaches, that guides you, that loves you, that embraces you. The power is real! *You already know it to be true* or you wouldn't waste your time here. It's very much like the expert highdiver who runs to the edge of the board and hesitates—he knows the water is there and he knows that he can do it, it's just that he is waiting for his moment. So what we do, my friends, is sit here on Sunday and we talk, and then you go home and do whatever it is you do, until one moment all of your energy is amassed and you leap! So I enjoy, in the vernacular, 'hanging around' with you while you are waiting for your moment.

So, I would like to talk of a truth from my side of the Light. Please hear me. You have been told that this is the kindergarten of the universe, that somehow you are children, somehow you are not quite as vast as others. I would like to tell you my perception. You have taken on one of the most difficult jobs in the Createdness, which is this—to be able to feel the lightest, most ephemeral energy vortex which you call God on a planet that is one of the densest in the Createdness. *I call that courageous.* The Divine has to make Itself felt in all parts of Creation. By choosing human form and valiantly attempting to awaken and experience the direct feeling of that illusive Power in the density of this planet is absolutely amazing. You do not have to make excuses for your experiment. The job is clear. You understood it when you came. When you feel the Divine in the density of this planet, you increase the power that surrounds it. This planet is on an evolutionary journey and every time one of you connects with the Divine and feels that Power, you increase the chances of everyone else experiencing the same by that extent. The truth is that this is one of the most valiant experiments in all creation and I ask you to honor it. The Divine has to be felt in every part and that is your job. And I would like to thank you, because in my reaches of consciousness I do travel to other places and their efforts are different, but *nowhere* have I seen any effort more valiant. This is why I can say that this particular expression of Divine Power is honored throughout the Universe. So please remember, it is a difficult job and I honor your striving. I honor your decision not to take your awareness to a less demanding job. Know that it is working. *It is working.* So, thank you. And thank you all for coming.

Production
Gary Mack

Word Processing
Janet Zanna
Phyllis Johnson

Typesetting
WD Type, Taos, NM

Informal tapes and transcripts of talks
by Bartholomew are available from
Dr. John Aiken
P.O. Box 1183
Socorro, NM 87801